★ GREAT WORLD WAR II PROJECTS ★

YOU CAN BUILD YOURSELF

Sheri Bell-Rehwoldt

nomad press

DEDICATION

To Christy, Emily, Kaitlyn, Sam, Jon, Gabe, Christian, Joshua, Amanda, and Nick.
May you grow up to appreciate the determination, faith, focus, and sacrifices
of the Americans who truly earned the reputation of being
"the greatest generation on earth."

Nomad Press
A division of Nomad Communications
10 9 8 7 6 5 4 3 2

This book was manufactured by Sheridan Books,
Ann Arbor, MI USA.
Job # 336101
ISBN: 978-0-977129-41-6

Questions regarding the ordering of this book should be addressed to
Independent Publishers Group
814 N. Franklin St.
Chicago, IL 60610
www.ipgbook.com

Nomad Press
2456 Christian St.
White River Junction, VT 05001
www.nomadpress.net

Contents

IMPORTANT PEOPLE

Adolf Hitler: The German dictator who started World War II to create a great German state for all Germans. He sought the destruction of all European Jews, millions of whom were killed in Nazi death camps. In 1945, Hitler committed suicide in his underground bunker in Berlin as Allied troops approached.

Sir Winston Churchill: As prime minister of Britain, Churchill was able to inspire the British people to great patriotism. This gave them the courage to deal with the physical dangers and sacrifices demanded of them during the war.

Franklin D. Roosevelt: America's 32nd president, Roosevelt was known as FDR. Before the United States entered the war on December 8, 1941, Roosevelt helped Britain, the Soviet Union, France, and other countries fighting Germany by providing all kinds of supplies through his 1941 Lend-Lease Act. Roosevelt died before the end of the war, in April 1945.

A meeting between Stalin, Roosevelt, and Churchill in 1943 at the Russian Embassy in Teheran, Iran.

Dwight D. Eisenhower: An army general, Eisenhower served as the supreme commander of the Allied Expeditionary Forces in Europe during World War II. He planned the invasion of France known as Operation Overlord, which helped the Allies to defeat Hitler. Eisenhower later served as America's 34th president.

Joseph Stalin: The dictator of the Soviet Union from 1928 through World War II and until he died in 1953. Stalin is credited with transforming the Soviet Union into a superpower. He was also responsible for the deaths of millions of his own people who were sent to harsh labor camps, mostly accused of being enemies of the state. After Hitler invaded the Soviet Union, Stalin sided with Britain and was one of the Allied powers.

Benito Mussolini: A fascist, Mussolini ruled Italy from 1922 to 1943 through intimidation and total control of the media and military. During World War II he sided with Nazi Germany.

General Hideki Tojo: Japan's prime minister during most of the war (until July 1944). Tojo commanded the Japanese military and ordered the attack on Pearl Harbor on December 7, 1941. After Japan surrendered to the Allied forces in 1945, Tojo shot himself before being arrested by the U.S. military. He survived but was executed as a war criminal in 1948.

Harry S. Truman: Truman became America's 33rd president when President Roosevelt died. It was his decision to drop two atomic bombs on Japan, which quickly brought an end to World War II.

Mussolini and Hitler

Churchill and Eisenhower

WORLD WAR II TIMELINE

⭐ **1939**

—**August 1939** The Soviet Union and Germany sign a nonaggression pact, agreeing not to fight each other when they both invade Poland.

—**September 1939** Hitler invades Poland from the west. France, Great Britain, Australia, New Zealand, Canada, South Africa, and India declare war on Germany. This is the official start to World War II. The countries against Germany are called the Allies. The Soviet Union invades Poland from the east.

—**October 1939** Poland surrenders to Hitler. The Nazis begin persecuting Polish Jews.

—**November 1939** The United States begins selling military supplies to Britain and France. Meanwhile, the Soviet Union attacks Finland.

⭐ **1940**

—**April 1940** Germany invades Denmark and Norway, and Denmark surrenders.

—**May 1940** Germany invades Belgium, the Netherlands, Luxembourg, and France. Winston Churchill becomes Britain's new prime minister. Belgium and the Netherlands surrender.

—**June 1940** Italy enters the war on the side of Nazi Germany, declaring war on France and Britain. France and Norway surrender.

—**July 1940** Churchill rejects a peace pact proposed by Hitler. The Battle of Britain begins when Germany starts bombing Britain.

—**September–October 1940** Germany intensely bombs London. This "blitz" continues for 57 nights, killing more than 40,000 citizens. The bombing of London continues off and on until the following May, but Britain fends off Germany's attacks and Hitler is unable to invade. Japan joins Italy and Germany in fighting the Allies. This is known as the Tripartite Pact, and the three countries are called the Axis Powers.

⭐ 1941

March 1941 The United States continues to send military equipment and other supplies to the Allies but no longer requires payment, at least not until after the war.

June 1941 Germany invades the Soviet Union, violating the nonaggression pact Germany signed with the Soviet Union in 1939. The invasion was called Operation Barbarossa.

July 1941 The Soviet Union joins the Allies.

December 1941 Japan attacks Pearl Harbor, an American naval base in Hawaii, along with other Allied bases in the Pacific and Asia. The United States and Britain declare war on Japan. Germany and Italy declare war on the United States.

⭐ 1942

January–February 1942 The Nazis organize their "final solution," the complete extermination of European Jews in death camps. Japanese troops take control of large portions of East Asia and the Pacific, including Hong Kong, Singapore, the Philippines, Thailand, Malaysia, and Burma.

February 1942 President Roosevelt signs Executive Order 9066, allowing the internment of Japanese Americans, as well as German and Italian Americans and other foreigners.

June 1942 The United States wins the Battle of Midway, a major turning point in the war in the Pacific.

December 1942 Scientists in the United States work on an atomic bomb.

⭐ 1943

July 1943 Mussolini is removed from power by the Italian king. Italy begins secret peace talks with the Allies.

September 1943 Italy surrenders to the Allies.

October 1943 Italy declares war on Germany.

November 1943 Churchill, Roosevelt, and Stalin meet in Teheran, Iran, to discuss Operation Overlord, the Allied invasion of Normandy, France, against Germany's army.

⭐ 1944

January 1944 General Dwight D. Eisenhower takes charge of planning Operation Overlord.

June 1944 Allied forces launch Operation Overlord. They land at Normandy on June 6, known as D-day. In heavy fighting the Allies gradually push the Germans back towards Germany. Over the following months, city after city in Europe is liberated by the Allies as the Germans retreat.

July 1944 The entire Japanese government resigns.

August 1944 Paris is liberated by Allied troops.

November 1944 Roosevelt is elected to his fourth term as U.S. president. He was the only president to serve more than two terms.

⭐ 1945

January 1945 Auschwitz, a Nazi death camp in Poland, is liberated. The Americans defeat the Germans in the Battle of the Bulge.

February 1945 The Unites States takes the Pacific island of Iwo Jima in a bloody battle memorialized in a famous photo of six marines raising the American flag. Churchill, Roosevelt, and Stalin meet in Yalta to discuss the end of the war and how to divide up Germany.

April 1945 Roosevelt dies. Vice President Harry S. Truman is sworn in as president. Mussolini is captured and executed by Italian partisans. Hitler commits suicide in his Berlin bunker.

May 1945 Germany surrenders on May 7. Truman declares May 8 V-E Day (Victory in Europe).

August 1945 The United States drops atomic bombs on the Japanese cities of Hiroshima (August 6) and Nagasaki (August 9). The Soviet Union declares war on Japan. Japan's Emperor Hirohito accepts the Allies' terms of surrender on August 14. This becomes known as V-J Day (Victory over Japan).

World War II Europe

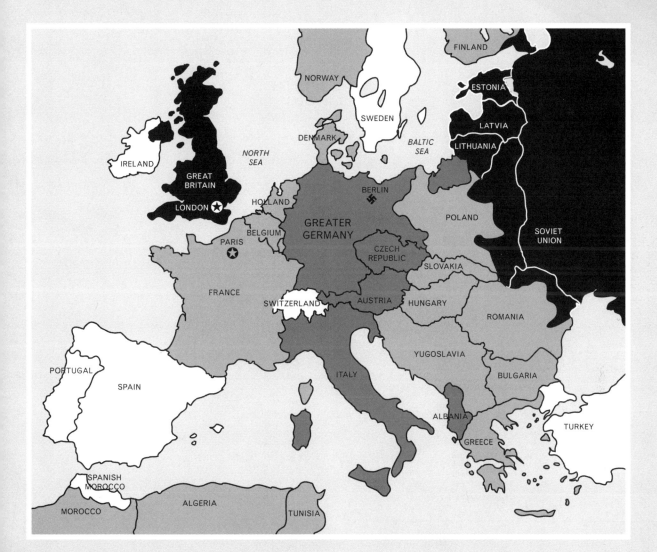

Allies

Axis powers, August 1939

Extent of Axis control, May 1941

Neutral nations

World War II South Pacific

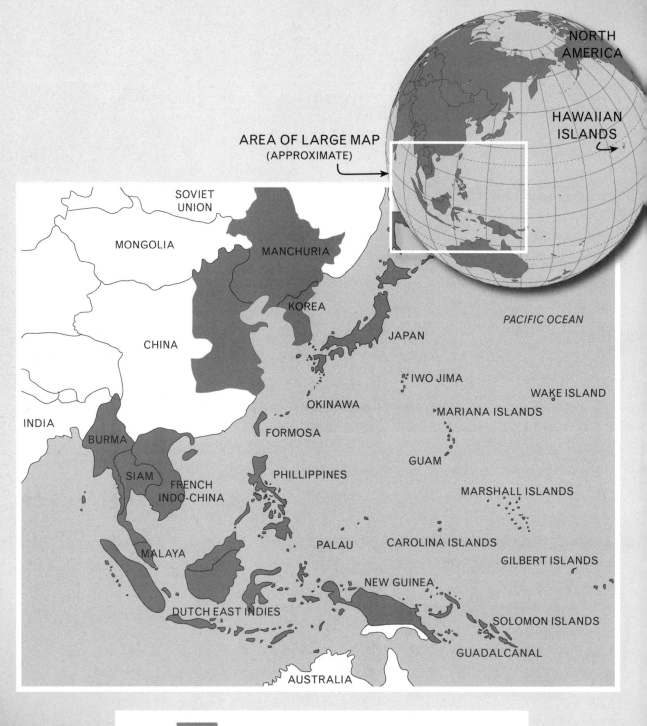

NORTH AMERICA

HAWAIIAN ISLANDS

AREA OF LARGE MAP
(APPROXIMATE)

SOVIET UNION

MONGOLIA

MANCHURIA

KOREA

CHINA

JAPAN

PACIFIC OCEAN

IWO JIMA

OKINAWA

WAKE ISLAND

MARIANA ISLANDS

INDIA

BURMA

FORMOSA

GUAM

SIAM

FRENCH INDO-CHINA

PHILLIPPINES

MARSHALL ISLANDS

MALAYA

PALAU

CAROLINA ISLANDS

GILBERT ISLANDS

NEW GUINEA

DUTCH EAST INDIES

SOLOMON ISLANDS

GUADALCANAL

AUSTRALIA

Japanese Empire 1942

Introduction

⭐ **Have you ever thought about what life would be like if you had lived** during World War II? This was a very difficult period in world history, when many people around the globe were at war with each other. Countries demanded total patriotism and cooperation from their citizens during the war. It was a time of fear, determination, sacrifice, and longing. For some, particularly the Jews and other "enemies" of the **Nazis** living in German-occupied Europe, the war years were particularly cruel. Their rights as human beings were swept aside, their property was taken, and many of them were murdered or worked to death in Nazi prison camps. Life was also dangerous and difficult in areas taken over by the Japanese in Asia and the Pacific. And yet, the war years also gave people opportunities to offer their best. Many risked their lives to help others.

This book will help you discover what life was like during World War II for soldiers in the field and for their families back home. You'll learn, for example, why Americans held scrap drives, why they were issued ration coupons, and how women proved they could do a man's job just fine. Find out about the people, places, and events of World

Know Your **World War II Words**

Nazi: a member of the National Socialist German Worker's Party, led by Adolf Hitler

Allies: Great Britain, France, the Soviet Union, and the United States, who were allied against Italy, Japan, and Germany

Axis: Germany, Italy, and Japan during WWII

democracy: government by the people based on equality and majority rule

fascism: government by a dictator, who rules through terror and control over everything in society

dictator: an absolute ruler who is harsh and oppressive

War II, including how the **Allied** armies fooled the Germans, and how balloons protected cities from low-flying bombers. See how technology gave the United States an edge, and the critical roles played by spies and code breakers. Discover the names for British bomb shelters and the names of two Americans who worked for the Germans and Japanese as radio personalities to try to discourage American troops. You'll create projects that will give you an idea of what people did during the war to make do, have fun, and support the troops. Most of the projects in this book can be made by kids with minimal adult supervision, and the supplies needed are either common household items or easily available at craft stores. So, take a step back into the 1940s and get ready to **Build It Yourself**.

HOW IT ALL BEGAN

★ **World War II isn't the only war in history that involved countries all over** the world. In fact, it came only 20 years after World War I, which was fought between 1914 and 1918. Called "the Great War" and "the war to end all wars," governments all over Europe agreed that a war as bloody as that one should never happen again. But just two decades later, World War II officially began when German troops marched into Poland on September 1, 1939. How did the world go from peace to war again so quickly?

It was because of Adolf Hitler, the dictator of Germany. In 1933, Hitler was the leader of the National Socialist German Worker's Party. Known as the Nazi party, it won more votes than the other political parties in Germany, which was still a democracy at the time. Hitler managed to take over the government after having his opponents arrested and killed. Despite using violence, Hitler won the support of many German people by promising that he would make them a strong and powerful nation. In fact, Hitler told the German people that they were a superior race and that, under his leadership, they would experience a thousand years of prosperity, with plenty of food and work. Why did the Germans listen to Hitler?

These promises rallied the German people, who felt a deep shame after losing World War I. Daily life in Germany following the First World War had been very hard for most people because of soaring **inflation** caused by Germany's growing debt. The winners of World War I required the German government to pay huge **reparations**. Germany didn't have enough money. Inflation happens when the prices of things rise, so money isn't worth as much. The prices of food and other items rose so high in Germany that most people could not buy them. People had to carry their money in wheel bar-

Adolf Hitler

rows—if they had any. Their money became nearly worthless! Many lives were ruined. German citizens became pessimistic, and many who suffered during this time turned to Hitler and the Nazi Party. He was the only one who promised to solve Germany's problems. This helped Hitler to move in and gain power.

A political poster supporting Hitler.

The Treaty of Versailles, which was the formal agreement that ended World War I, forced Germany (and Germany's allies) to accept full responsibility for causing the war. Germany was not allowed to have a large military. But Hitler had his eye on world domination. He worked to revoke the treaty when he came to power in 1933. He ordered the creation, expansion, and modernization of the German air force, navy, and army. By 1939, Germany had the world's second largest military force—lagging only behind the Soviet Union. In comparison, the U.S. military ranked 18 in

Know Your World War II Words

inflation: the rise in the prices of things

reparations: payment of damages

storm troopers: the Nazi militia, known for violence and brutality

concentration camps: prison camps known for very harsh conditions

the world! Creating a strong military would become America's most important goal as war spread across Europe and Asia.

While Hitler promised good things for German citizens, there was one group of people he purposely excluded: Jews. Hitler hated Jewish people. He blamed them for all of Germany's problems. Many German people were willing to believe that Hitler was right. German children were taught to despise Jews. German boys had to join the Hitler Youth and girls had to join the League of German Girls. In these youth clubs, children between the ages of 10 and 18 learned to view Jews as their enemy. The Nuremberg Laws of 1935 took away Jewish rights of German citizenship. In 1938, Jewish children were forced to leave public schools. Jews were also forbidden from entering non-Jewish businesses, restaurants, and movie theaters.

On the night of November 9, 1938, Nazi **storm troopers** burned hundreds of Jewish synagogues and destroyed or vandalized many Jewish-owned stores in Germany and German-occupied territories. (Germany had already taken over Austria and part of Czechoslovakia without firing a shot.) This night of terror is called Kristallnacht, "the Night of Broken Glass." More than 20,000 Jewish men were rounded up by the Nazis and police and sent to **concentration camps**.

Hitler: Prophet of Hate

"In the course of my life I have very often been a prophet, and have usually been ridiculed for it. During the time of my struggle for power it was in the first instance only the Jewish race that received my prophecies with laughter when I said that I would one day take over the leadership of the State, and with it that of the whole nation, and that I would then among other things settle the Jewish problem. Their laughter was uproarious, but I think that for some time now they have been laughing on the other side of their face. Today I will once more be a prophet: if the international Jewish financiers in and outside Europe should succeed in plunging the nations once more into a world war, then the result will not be the Bolshevizing of the earth, and thus the victory of Jewry, but the annihilation of the Jewish race in Europe!"

—Adolf Hitler, in a speech he made on January 30, 1939.

An anti-Semitic poster.

In September 1941, the Nazis issued yellow Star of David patches to all Jews living in Germany and German-occupied areas. Jews had to wear the patches on their outer clothing on the left side of their chest. If Jews were caught in public without the patch or their identification papers, they were fined or beaten. The patches created an "us versus them" mindset. Yet the Nazis weren't satisfied with terrorizing and humiliating the Jews. They wanted them removed completely.

The Nazis held a special conference in January 1942 to determine the "final solution" for the millions of Jews living in German-occupied Europe. The Nazis decided that all Jews should be killed. The term for the mass murder of Jews by the Nazis is "the **Holocaust**."

So they sent Jewish men, women, and children to labor and death camps, called concentration camps, in overcrowded railroad cars. Many Jews were killed right away in gas chambers. Those who were spared lived in horrible, overcrowded conditions. They received very little food, and were made to work long hours doing hard physical labor. In total, more than 6 million European Jews, as well as other persecuted groups such as gypsies, communists, and homosexuals, met their end in the Nazi camps.

One of the reasons Hitler wanted to get rid of the Jews and other groups that were "enemies" of Germany was to have more land for German citizens. Hitler felt it was his right to take the land of Poland and the Soviet Union to make room, what he called lebensraum (living room), for his "superior race." He began his conquest of Europe by invading Austria in 1938. He invaded Czechoslovakia in 1938–1939 and Poland in 1939. In 1940 his troops marched into Denmark, Norway, Belgium, Luxembourg, the Netherlands, and France. Hitler then surprised Soviet dictator Joseph Stalin by invading the Soviet Union in 1941, breaking an agreement he had signed just

★ WWII trivia ★

In the Tripartite Pact, Germany, Italy, and Japan agreed to stand by each other for the next 10 years, and to support each other if attacked by a country not yet involved in the war. Since Japan attacked the U.S. first, Germany was not obliged to help Japan when America struck back. Hitler did so anyway.

Hitler's superior race.

2 years earlier. Within Germany the Nazis imprisoned or executed all who opposed them, limiting the rights of German citizens and freedom of the press. Though President Franklin D. Roosevelt hoped the United States could stay out of the war, he helped those fighting Hitler by sending supplies and equipment.

By 1941 most Americans knew that the United States would eventually have to enter the war. But no one was prepared for the tragic event that forced the United States into it overnight. On the morning of December 7, 1941, hundreds of Japanese aircraft attacked Pearl Harbor, a U.S. naval base in Hawaii. The U.S. military was alerted by radar that bombers were approaching, but everyone thought the planes were American bombers! That's how unexpected the attack was. Within minutes, Japanese bombs rained down on sailors and civilians. In only an hour, close to 20 U.S. Navy ships were destroyed and almost 3,000 Americans were killed. Fortunately for the U.S. military, the U.S. aircraft-carrier fleet was not in Pearl Harbor at the time so it was not destroyed.

The very next day, on December 8, 1941, the United States formally declared war on Japan. The United States, Britain, and the Soviet Union, already known as the Allies, joined forces. They concentrated on winning the war against Germany, Italy, and Japan. These three countries had partnered together as the Axis powers on September 27, 1940, in an agreement called the Tripartite Pact.

Why did Japan attack the United States? For many years Japan had been expanding gradually, taking over parts of China and other countries in Asia. Japan was a small, crowded country. Like Germany, Japan wanted more territory. The military in Japan was very powerful and the government did what it said.

Fear struck the hearts of many Americans. If Japanese planes could reach Hawaii, could Japan attack California? Some citizens worried that the Japanese Americans living on the West Coast might be spies. Maybe they had even

WWII INVENTIONS

Radar

The British government patented radar in April 1935 based on the work of Sir Robert Alexander Watson-Watt, a physicist who developed a device to detect airplanes before they could be seen. He used high-frequency radio waves that bounced off the airplanes and identified their position. Watson-Wyatt called this device radio detecting and ranging (radar). Soon, the British government built radar stations along Britain's south coast to watch for enemy aircraft. The stations helped Britain win the Battle of Britain in 1940. In 1941 Watson-Watt traveled to the United States to help set up a radar system there.

U.S.S. Shaw exploding during the Japanese raid on Pearl Harbor, December 7, 1941.

helped Japan to launch the attack on Pearl Harbor! To calm people's fears, President Roosevelt allowed the army to force Japanese residents, many of whom had lived in the United States for 20 or 30 years, or even more, into guarded internment camps. These were nothing like the labor or death camps of the Nazis, but the internment camps were still difficult places to live. It was still prison. Most Japanese Americans were not allowed to leave until the end of 1944. When the government closed the camps, Japanese Americans looked forward to returning to their homes. But many who did so found their homes and businesses vandalized. Sometimes local residents were unwilling to welcome the Japanese Americans back. It took many years for Japanese Americans to rebuild their lives and their businesses. Some never did.

Even before it entered the war, the United States was rushing to rebuild its military. This was a huge challenge! Factories stopped making their peacetime products in order to produce planes, boats, jeeps, tanks, trucks, guns, and all kinds of other war supplies. Many men left their jobs to enter the military, so millions of women entered the workforce. Children, too, joined the war effort. They collected goods for scrap drives. Across America, citizens were asked to make sacrifices so that U.S. **troops** would have all they needed to win the war. Americans did so willingly, even when food, clothing, and gasoline became severely **rationed**.

Despite the enormous efforts of the United States and the huge addition of American troops and weapons, Hitler seemed unstoppable. The Allies realized they would have to force Hitler to fight on two fronts. Germany was already fighting the Russians to the east. The Allies decided to invade Normandy, France, attacking the Germans from the west. They wanted to force Hitler to fight the Allies to his east and west. Otherwise

Japanese American children awaiting internment.

they knew Hitler would have no obstacle to his goal of conquering Europe. On June 6, 1944, under the control of General Dwight D. Eisenhower, the supreme commander of the Allied Expeditionary Force in Europe, the Allies landed on five beaches in Normandy, codenamed Omaha, Utah, Juno, Sword, and Gold. It was the largest seaborne assault in history.

This attack was called Operation Overlord and it was huge: more than 6,000 ships, 12,000 planes, and 133,000 troops arrived on June 6. The Allies brought many specialized weapons for this assault. These included flame-throwing tanks, "flail" tanks that cleared land mines planted under the sand, amphibious trucks that drove soldiers and supplies up the beach, and gas masks, in case the Germans met them with poisonous gas.

D-day landing on the beach in Normandy.

While the invasion was no secret, the Germans were still fooled by the Allies—they thought the Allies were going to cross the English Channel into the French city of Pas-de-Calais. So the Germans had most of their military power there. What fooled the Germans into guarding Pas-de-Calais more heavily than Normandy? First, the Allies used fake airfields and placed inflatable rubber tanks and barges in areas of England nearest to Calais. These made it look like the Allies were gearing up for an attack. Second, the Allies parachuted hundreds of homing pigeons into Calais. The pigeons carried a message that asked anyone who found the birds to return them to England with information about German troops. The Allies used the information they received to help plan their attack. And third, the Allies parachuted hundreds of dummy paratroopers near Calais, which further confused the Germans.

Operation Overlord was still a bloody battle that lasted over 2 months, until August 19. Many Allied soldiers were killed by the Germans as they came onto the beach. But with luck and determination on their side, the brave Allied troops finally managed to secure the beaches and move inland. Hitler retaliated by attacking London with a weapon the Allies had never seen: the V-1, 26-foot-long, low-flying, pilotless bomb called "buzz bomb" or "doodlebug" because of its distinctive sound. Even with this and other new weapons, the Nazis couldn't win. Within 11 months of **D-day**, Allied troops were able to defeat Nazi Germany. On April 30, 1945, with thousands of Soviet soldiers and tanks closing in on his **bunker** in Berlin, Hitler killed himself. Hitler's dreams for German domination officially came to an end when General Eisenhower declared Victory in Europe Day (V-E Day) on May 8, 1945.

Unfortunately, World War II was not over yet. The Allies still fought the Japanese in the Pacific. And they kept fighting until Harry S. Truman, who became America's 33rd president when President Roosevelt died, authorized the dropping of two atomic bombs on Japan in August 1945. Japan surrendered on August 15, 1945, which is now commemorated in the United States each year as Victory over Japan day (V-J Day). When they heard that the war was finally over, more than two million ecstatic Americans celebrated the Axis defeat in New York City's Times Square. Tons of paper and confetti rained down on them from office windows.

This famous kiss took place in New York City's Times Square on August 15, 1945, when Japan announced its unconditional surrender.

Millions of soldiers and civilians from around the world died in World War II. In the United States alone, 15 million men and 200,000 women served in the military. More than 400,000 Americans were killed, more than 600,000 were wounded, and more than 100,000 were taken as prisoners of war or declared missing. With close to 60 million people killed in this global war, it was the bloodiest war in history.

Know Your World War II Words

troops a group of soldiers

rationing: to restrict consumption of something that is in short supply

D-day: the first day of any military operation, D-day of Operation Overload is the most famous

bunker: an underground fortified shelter

Crowds gather in Times Square to celebrate V-J Day, August 15, 1945.

ON THE HOME FRONT

★ **When the United States entered World War II in** December 1941, U.S. citizens had no idea how long the war would go on. Across the country, men were asked to join the military. Civilians were asked to "use up" and "do without." The government encouraged women to take over the millions of jobs left vacant by the men, which meant working 10, even 12-hour shifts. It also asked women to grow and can much of their own food and to make do without staples such as butter, chocolate, and red meat. Women were expected to help with **war bond** and **recycling drives**, volunteer with the **Red Cross**, and still take care of their children, as well as their homes and themselves. Many women who used to rely on maids had to do their own household chores when their maids took high-paying factory jobs. Women rose to the occasion, making their husbands, children, and country proud.

It is important to remember that American homes during World War II did not have air conditioning or central heat. People used coal or gas stoves to heat their houses. Most homes lacked washing machines, dishwashers, freezers, and televisions. Large supermarkets

"Use it up, wear it out, make it do, or do without."

SOLDIERS *without guns*

Know Your World War II Words

war bond: sold by the government to raise money for the war

recycling drive: organized collection of items to recycle into war supplies

Red Cross: an organization that cares for the sick, wounded, and homeless during wars and natural disasters

black market: an illegal market where rationed items are sold

propaganda: using information to promote a certain viewpoint

BUY WAR BONDS

LOOSE LIPS MIGHT Sink Ships

like we have today also did not yet exist, so people shopped in small specialty stores, such as butcher shops for meat and bakeries for bread.

Fortunately, the United States did not have to deal with frequent bomb raids like much of Europe did. Americans did experience shortages of food, clothing, and gasoline, though. The Office of Price Administration (OPA) set up rationing and price controls by 1942, so the United States would not experience the inflation and food shortages that occurred during World War I. Families were issued ration books to buy rationed items such as coffee, butter, chocolate, canned fruit, gasoline, oil, rubber, and shoes. But having a ration book did not guarantee that products would be available. Sometimes, store owners simply could not get the items. When they did, people quickly formed long lines to buy the goods before they ran out. Some people turned to the **black market** to get what they wanted. The term black market doesn't mean a specific place where goods were sold. It means the illegal practice of sell-

"Don't you know there's a war on?"

★ WWII trivia ★

Although bathrooms were installed in some homes after World War I, it wasn't until the late 1930s that rural areas had any indoor plumbing.

ing rationed or hard-to-find items at high prices. The government did not approve of black markets, and fined people it caught buying or selling goods this way.

The government used advertising to persuade American citizens to think and act in certain ways. Using information to cause or change behaviors and beliefs is called propaganda. All of the countries involved in World War II used **propaganda** to convince their citizens to remain patriotic and hate the enemy. Posters were displayed everywhere. They reminded Americans to conserve, ration, use up, report suspicious activity, black out their home and car lights, and view Germany and Japan as dangerous threats to American freedom.

WWII INVENTIONS

Ballpoint Pen

The ballpoint pen was invented by two brothers, Ladislao "Laszlo" and Georg Biro, as an improvement over the messy fountain pen. Laszlo, a journalist, and Georg, a chemist, made the ballpoint pen in 1938 to accommodate the thicker ink used by printing presses. During World War II, the British government bought the licensing rights to the ballpoint pen so that it could give its fighter pilots a pen that did not leak at high altitudes.

Advertisers, too, spent a lot of money reminding citizens to "do their share" after the government decided that companies didn't have to pay tax on ads that had a wartime theme. Companies also did a lot of advertising to keep their products on people's minds—even if they couldn't manufacture them during the war. Car manufacturers, for example, used advertising to promise that after the war life would be good with their new models.

Even with a war going on, Americans still found plenty of ways to have fun. Movies were very popular, as was baseball, dancing, boxing, roller skating, bowling, and reading. Although television had been invented before World War II, very few people owned them. They had to rely on radio for their news and entertainment in the home. Families gathered nightly around their living room radios to tune in to their favorite programs, such as *The Lone Ranger* and *Abbott and Costello*. Every few months President Roosevelt

Group gathered around the office radio, V-J Day.

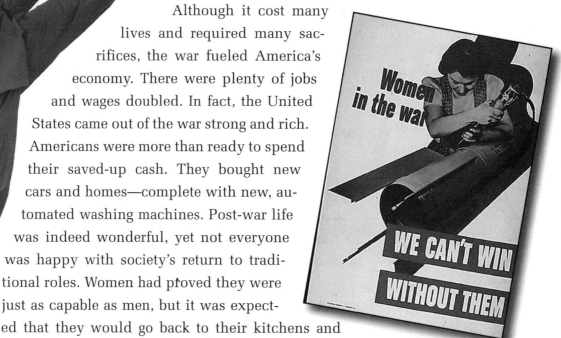

talked to Americans about the war through radio addresses he called *Fireside Chats*. People also got news from newspapers, magazines, and war reels that were shown before Hollywood movies. The most widely read war correspondent was a journalist named Ernie Pyle. More than 12 million readers were fascinated by his accounts of the war. His detailed descriptions of soldiers' lives appeared six times a week in more than 300 newspapers. Pyle was killed by the Japanese in 1945, during a battle on the island of Ie Shima.

Although it cost many lives and required many sacrifices, the war fueled America's economy. There were plenty of jobs and wages doubled. In fact, the United States came out of the war strong and rich. Americans were more than ready to spend their saved-up cash. They bought new cars and homes—complete with new, automated washing machines. Post-war life was indeed wonderful, yet not everyone was happy with society's return to traditional roles. Women had proved they were just as capable as men, but it was expected that they would go back to their kitchens and low-paying jobs, so that men could return to their pre-war jobs. Again, the government used propaganda to direct behavior. A woman is a substitute, claimed a War Department brochure, like plastic instead of metal. Still, women took great pride knowing that the Allies could not have won the war without their many contributions.

Women in the war

WE CAN'T WIN WITHOUT THEM

LIVING IN
FEAR

After Japan bombed Pearl Harbor on December 7, 1941, Americans were afraid there would be more air attacks. Children practiced air-raid drills in school. They learned to hide under their desks if the air-raid siren sounded. Families practiced air-raid drills at home, and assembled air-raid kits in case they were told to run to their cellars. The kits contained basic items such as blankets, candles, jugs of water, food, a shovel, and a radio.

To help protect against the threat of aerial attacks, the U.S. military quickly trained volunteers to spot enemy aircraft. As many as 600,000 American civilians served as aircraft spotters at 14,000 observation posts along the U.S. coast as part of the Ground Observer Corps. These men, women, and teenagers memorized the shapes of U.S. and enemy planes by studying identification cards. They watched the skies during many long hours. Even blind people acted as spotters. They reported every time they heard a plane pass overhead.

Residents blacked out their windows at night with black paint or heavy curtains. They did this so bomber

★ WWII trivia ★

American children built 500,000 model airplanes that were used to train aircraft spotters to recognize the difference between American and enemy planes. The military also issued spotter playing cards to help soldiers and civilians to identify planes.

Sending Kids to Safety

British parents who lived in cities feared for the safety of their children during German air raids. Many parents sent their kids to live with families in the country. Because America was much safer than Europe, some parents tried to send their children to the United States for the rest of the war. To arrange for the care of these refugee children, an American activist and Quaker, Clarence Pickett, formed the United States Committee for the Care of European Children in the summer of 1940. One of the Committee's strongest supporters was First Lady Eleanor Roosevelt, the wife of the president of the United States. She supported the 1940 Wagner-Rogers Bill, which proposed rescue efforts for European Jewish children refugees. If this bill had passed, it would have allowed 20,000 Jewish children to enter the United States. But because the public resisted any involvement in the war at that time the bill did not pass. Still, several hundred Jewish children managed to enter the United States in 1942 and 1943.

Families in Britain building Anderson Shelters.

pilots wouldn't be able to easily target American cities. On the East Coast it was important the cities did not light up the horizon, silouetting merchant shipping. This would have made the ships easy targets.

Many women served as air-raid wardens. It was their job to help the fire and police departments put out lights during a blackout. They were also in charge of getting medical help if any areas were bombed. Fortunately, further attacks like the one on Pearl Harbor did not occur. During these "blackout" periods, stores darkened their windows, and street lights were turned off or painted black. Cities and towns across America were in total darkness at night. This made it a challenge for people to see where they were going. Some companies rushed to develop blackout products, such as lighted walking canes, hoping to make lots of sales.

Citizens were also required to turn off their car lights, but the government soon allowed Americans to make light shields (called eyelashes) for their headlights, or to paint the tops of their headlights black. This directed the light down toward the road, giving people just enough light to see in front of them. Drivers were restricted to a speed limit of only 35 miles per hour. This helped to prevent accidents. Although the slower speed limit was inconvenient and made travel time longer, it helped to extend the life of vehicle tires. This was good for conserving resources for the war effort.

British citizens also experienced blackout periods—and faced many devastating German air raids. In one way, they were prepared. After the German Army mobilized in the summer of 1938, the British government began distributing metal shelters to the British people, called Anderson Shelters. These shelters were designed to be partially buried in backyards as protection against possible air raids. Nearly 200,000 Anderson Shelters were distributed before Britain declared war on Germany on September 3, 1939. More than 2 million were built during the war. The shelters were 6 feet high, 4½ feet wide, and 6½ feet long. Each could fit six people. The roofs of the shelters were made from six curved panels that were bolted together. Three straight sheets formed each side of the shelter, and the front and back were made out of two more straight panels. A door was cut in one end.

On July 10, 1940, the shelters were put to the test. The **German Luftwaffe** began dropping bombs on the British in an attempt to wipe out its military. This fight between Britain and Germany is known as the Battle of Britain. During the battle, on September 7, 1940, Hitler ordered a **blitz** on London after Britain dropped bombs on the German city of Berlin. The bombs rained down on the British for 57 consecutive nights during **the Blitz**. In total, the Germans dropped 35,000 tons of bombs on London and other British cities.

The Anderson Shelters may have helped British citizens feel safer, but they were very uncomfortable to spend the night in. Much of each shelter was buried below ground, so they were quite damp and tended to flood. Even though the shelter's roof was covered with at least 15 inches of soil, which was often used for growing vegetables, the shelters

⭐ WWII trivia ⭐

The British government believed that the Axis powers planned to use poison gas on Britain's civilian population, so it gave gas masks to everyone living in Britain. By 1940, the British government issued 38 million gas masks. Adult gas masks were black, but children were given colorful versions called Mickey Mouse masks.

Know Your
World War II Words

German Luftwaffe: the German airforce

blitz: an intense, all-out attack

The Blitz: the 1940 bombing of London and other British cities

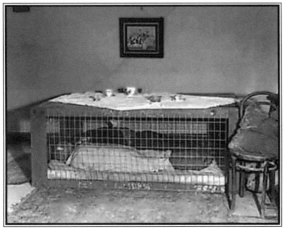

Morrison Shelter in a home.

could not drown out the sound of the bombs screaming overhead.

People who did not have yard space for Anderson Shelters took their chances in their homes. Many spent nights in crowded public shelters and stuffy underground railway stations. When the British government became worried about the overcrowding in these spaces, it developed an indoor shelter called the Morrison Shelter. By the end of 1941, half a million Morrison Shelters had been distributed to British civilians. These shelters were a definite improvement over the Anderson Shelter. They were placed in people's living rooms, where people could climb in and stay warm and dry. Constructing the shelters was complicated though, because each kit had 359 parts.

Did they look much different from Anderson Shelters? Yes. They were lower, and looked like large animal cages. The top of the shelter was made of a solid 1/8-inch steel

★ WWII trivia ★

Some famous British landmarks damaged by German bombing include Buckingham Palace and Westminster Abbey.

plate, so that it would protect residents if chunks of their house fell on it. The side panels were welded wire mesh and lifted up so that people could crawl inside.

The shelter had enough space for three people to sleep. People tended to use them as tables because they took up so much of their living rooms—some even used them as Ping-Pong tables!

Hitler failed miserably in his plan to break the morale of the British people. The bombings actually united the British against their enemy. In the face of constant attack, the British adopted a motto of "Business as usual." They were intent on living their lives as close to normal as possible. The Battle of Britain finally ended when Hitler ordered the German pilots to turn their planes toward eastern Europe to invade the Soviet Union. This invasion is known as Operation Barbarossa.

OPERATION BARBAROSSA

Make Your Own
Anderson Shelter Model

Because this is just a model, you're making a very small version of the shelter. Think of the roasting pan (or baking pan) as a home's garden space.

1 Soften the flat bottom of the miniature loaf pan so that the square edges become rounded. This is easy to do with your fingers because the foil is so thin. Keep the sides of the pan straight. This pan is your shelter.

2 Cut a doorway in one end of the loaf pan. Make it big enough so you can see inside the shelter. Position the shelter in the garden space. You can fill the shelter with miniature doll furniture, such as a bed or a table and chairs, as well as people and pets, before you cover it with dirt. You may want to glue or tape the pieces down to make sure they do not shift when you move the model.

3 Surround your shelter with dirt or potting soil, burying the shelter about a half-inch. Pack the dirt down. Pack more dirt up the three closed sides and on the top of the shelter, so that it looks like a pile of dirt.

4 Use the parsley to fill in the dirt with "grass." Add other fresh or fake herbs and flowers, if you want to.

5 Show your model to your friends, explaining how the shelter was used during the war.

Inside an Anderson Shelter.

supplies

- ✪ **miniature foil loaf pan**
- ✪ **foil roasting pan OR a rectangular baking pan with sides that are at least 1 inch high, big enough to hold the miniature loaf pan and leave space for the garden**
- ✪ **dollhouse furniture, people, and pets**
- ✪ **scissors**
- ✪ **glue or tape**
- ✪ **potting soil or dirt**
- ✪ **parsley leaves for grass**
- ✪ **herbs and flowers**

Make Your Own
WWII Spotter Airplane Models

You're about to make four World War II planes from sheets of craft foam board. Your goal is to be able to identify each plane as American or British (friend), or German or Japanese (foe). Note how the wings and tail give each plane its unique shape.

Study the pattern provided for each plane on the following pages. Note the plane's signature markings. The American plane has stars, the British plane has bulls-eyes, the German plane has black crosses and swastikas, and the Japanese plane has circles.

1 Photocopy or trace each plane pattern, then cut up into separate pieces. You will have three pieces for each plane: the body, the wings, and the rudder. Select a foam color for each plane. Draw each plane pattern piece onto the foam, using the marker or pen. Cut the pieces out.

2 Using the pattern as a guide, add the plane's signature markings on the wings, tail, and body using your colored markers. If you want to add further details from the pattern, feel free! To see larger pictures of the planes and more detail, go to www.parmodels.com.

3 Use your scissors to carefully cut a slit in the plane's body, just under the cockpit area, for the wings. A small slit cut in the front of the wings will help stabilize your plane. Slide the wings through the slit until they sit balanced on either side of the body. Carefully cut a slit in the plane's tail section and rudder. Slide the rudder through the slit until it, too, is balanced. Use pieces of tape if necessary to hold everything together.

4 Once all the planes are complete, hold each one up and note how different they look from the side. Now hold each plane above your head. Note how the wing shapes are unique. When you're able to tell each plane apart, just by its shape and marking, consider yourself an expert spotter!

Note: *We would like to thank Paul Bradley for the use of his plane patterns. Go to www.parmodels.com.*

supplies

- ✪ paper
- ✪ scissors
- ✪ thin-tip marker or pen
- ✪ foam board in a different color for each plane
- ✪ colored markers
- ✪ tape

Here's a bit of history on each plane:

AMERICAN—North American P-51 Mustang

The P-51 was designed in 1940 at the request of the British.
During World War II, the P-51 Mustang proved its value as an
escort for high-altitude bombers. In fact, the flight crews of the B-17s
(the "Flying Fortress") and B-24s considered the Mustang an essen-
tial "little friend" as it performed so well at picking off Luftwaffe fighters. By the end of the
war, P-51s had destroyed nearly 5,000 enemy aircraft in the air, more than any other fighter in
Europe. The P-51 was dubbed the "Cadillac of the Sky."

BRITISH—Supermarine Spitfire

The Supermarine Spitfire was a single-seat fighter used by the
British Air Force and many Allied countries during World
War II. The Spitfire's elliptical wings gave it a very distinctive
look, while its thin cross-section gave the plane speed. Pilots loved this plane.
Some Spitfires even saw action into the 1950s.

GERMAN—Focke-Wulf FW 190

In 1938, the German Air Ministry decided to build another fighter
aircraft to supplement the Messerschmitt Bf109. Designers came
up with the Focke-Wulf FW 190, which become fully opera-
tional in July 1941. More than 20,000 were built during World
War II, and they became the best fighter planes in the Luftwaffe. Some British pilots even
acknowledged that the Focke-Wulf's speed and maneuverability allowed it to outperform their
own Supermarine Spitfire.

JAPANESE—Kawasaki Ki-61 Hien ("Tony")

The Kawasaki Ki-61 Hien was so different from other Japanese
planes that when Allied pilots first saw it they thought it was
a copy of an Italian fighter plane. They gave it the code name
"Tony." Though the Ki-61 was an excellent fighter and found early success
in combat against American fighters, it was outclassed by the end of the war.
About 3,000 were built, but few survived the war.

American:
North American P-51 Mustang

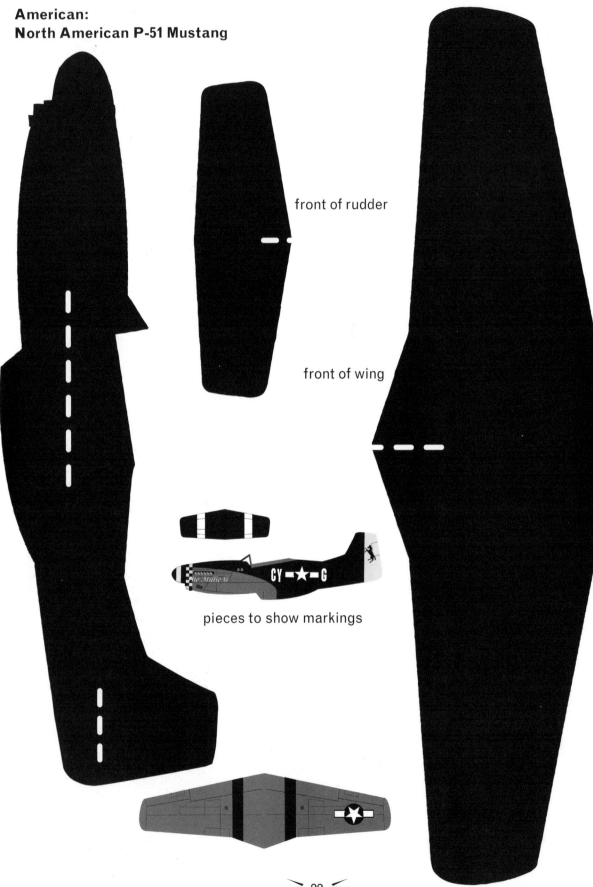

front of rudder

front of wing

pieces to show markings

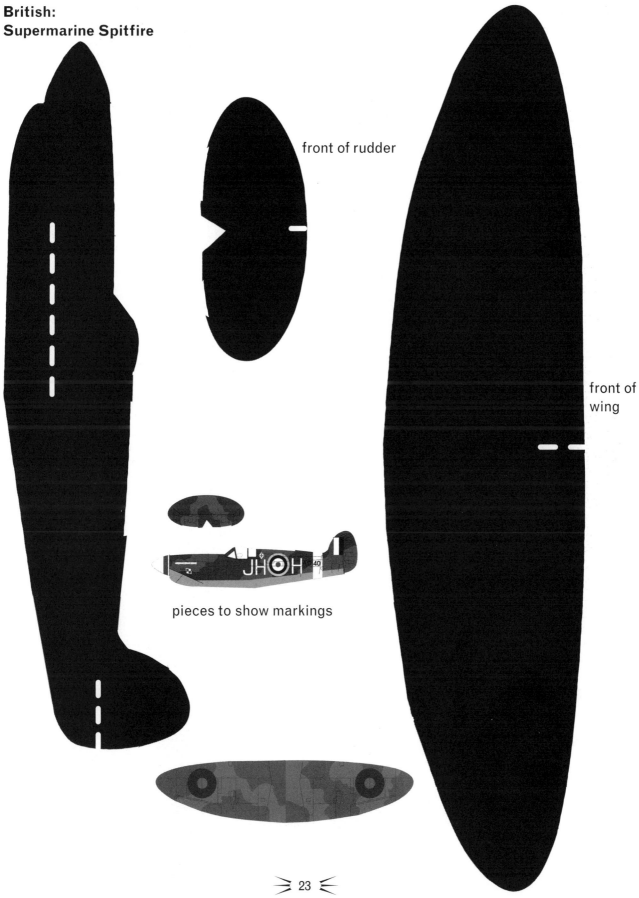

British:
Supermarine Spitfire

front of rudder

front of
wing

pieces to show markings

German:
Focke-Wulf FW 190

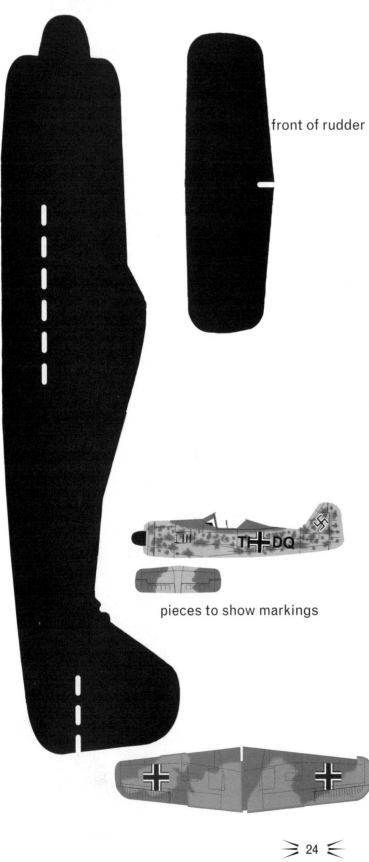

front of rudder

front of wing

pieces to show markings

Japanese:
Kawasaki Ki-61 Hien ("Tony")

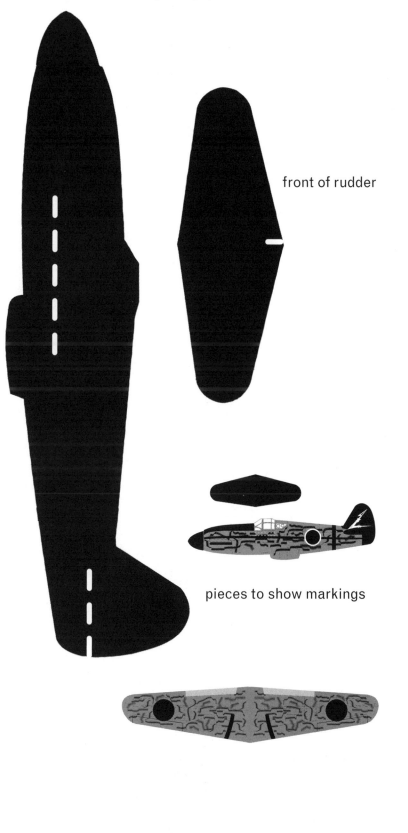

front of rudder

front of wing

pieces to show markings

SUPPORTING THE
TROOPS

★ **There is no time in American history more recognized for its patriotism** than during World War II. That's because every aspect of American life focused on a single goal: stopping the Axis powers. American families spent a lot of time trying to get by on less so that American soldiers could have more. And most jobs in the United States focused on making war supplies for the Allies.

By 1942, Italy, Germany, and Japan controlled most of Europe and the southwest Pacific. In order to fight them, President Franklin Roosevelt asked American companies to stop manufacturing peacetime products so they could churn out planes, anti-aircraft guns, tents, and boats. So instead of producing family cars on their assembly lines, automobile plants rolled out military jeeps and tanks. Rather than make women's nylon hosiery, factories turned nylon into parachutes and airplane tires.

Roosevelt soon needed more men for the fight, so the U.S. government **drafted** millions of American men into the military. With so many men leaving the workforce, American companies urgently needed to find new workers to keep up the production of war supplies. They turned to American women. Women who held low-paying jobs as waitresses, hairdressers, and maids, jumped at the

"I've found the job where I fit best!"

FIND YOUR WAR JOB
In Industry – Agriculture – Busin

chance to make more money and help their country by joining the workforce. Millions of middle-class housewives did too. School-age girls, young women, and mothers with sons on the front lines took jobs to earn extra cash and keep busy so they wouldn't worry as much about the safety of their brothers, husbands, and sons. Hanging up their housedresses, these women donned handkerchiefs as turbans, and overalls or slacks as they loaded shells or riveted or welded together planes and ships. They also sewed tents and parachutes. "Rosie the Riveter," a fictional character painted by American artist Norman Rockwell, became the nation's symbol for its strong female workforce. Outside of the factories, women drove taxis, operated cranes, ran farms, and worked as police and secretaries. In all, 6 million women joined the workforce during World War II.

Know Your World War II Words

draft: to recruit or force a person to serve in the armed forces

mandate: a command or order

Rosie the Riveter

Many men also worked in the war factories on the home front. They might have been turned down for military service because of a health problem or because of their age, but they certainly did their part to contribute. Many unskilled workers also found jobs. Assembly lines in factories meant that a worker had to learn only one task well. It was simple for employers to train new workers. America became a whiz at mass production and new technologies.

Many factories also hired people with disabilities. In fact, by 1943 nearly 200,000 people with disabilities worked for the war effort, up from 27,703 in 1940. Employers didn't care if people worked from wheelchairs, or if they were blind, as long as they could do their job on the assembly line.

Large numbers of temporary workers worked at different factories all over the

⭐ WWII trivia ⭐

Recycled toothpaste tubes provided tin for airplanes, while just one recycled refrigerator produced three machine guns.

Milkweed Pods for Life Vests

One way American children helped the war effort was to pick wild milkweed plants. Milkweed has large pods filled with little flexible fibers. The plants made excellent filler for life jackets when supplies of kapok were cut off by the Japanese. Like kapok, milkweed is a silky fiber that is both water resistant and floats. Kapok surrounds the seeds pods of the ceiba tree, which grows primarily in Asia. Just 1½ pounds of milkweed floss could keep a 150-pound sailor afloat for 10 hours. During 1944 and 1945, people collected more than 25 million pounds of wild milkweed pods. That's enough to fill 700 freight-train cars!

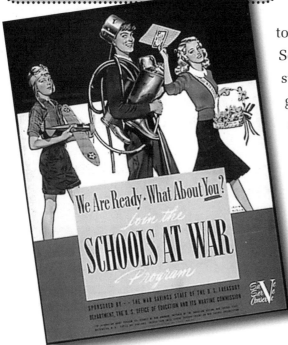

We Are Ready · What About You?
Join the
SCHOOLS AT WAR
Program

SPONSORED BY — THE WAR SAVINGS STAFF OF THE U. S. TREASURY
DEPARTMENT, THE U. S. OFFICE OF EDUCATION AND ITS WARTIME COMMISSION

⭐ WWII trivia ⭐

Little Orphan Annie, a popular comic-strip character, was used during the war to encourage children to participate in the war effort as Junior Commandos. Children who took the Junior Commando Pledge helped to collect scrap rubber and metal and saved their pennies to buy war bonds.

country. Unfortunately, these workers had to compete for a very limited supply of places to live. Local residents fought to keep new construction to a minimum. They were afraid that housing values would drop if there was too much available housing after the war. Many workers ended up sharing rooms in boarding houses, dormitories, apartments, and shacks—which they often could only occupy during certain hours. Imagine not being able to go to your room because someone else was sleeping there! Some of these temporary workers even had to live in horse stalls.

In February 1943, when there still weren't enough workers, President Roosevelt decided to **mandate** that people work 48 hours a week. Some women worked 50 or 60 hours a week—and still had to take care of their families when they got home. Many factories stayed open 24 hours a day. Factory workers who didn't have babysitters sometimes dropped off their children at nearby movie theaters, which also stayed open around the clock. Women often had to take days off from work when their children were sick, or when they heard rumors that rationed items might be available.

Surprisingly, by 1944 as many as 3 million kids, between the ages of 14 and 17, also held jobs in factories, supermarkets, drugstores, bowling alleys, and restaurants. Many worked long hours, even skipping school. Children also knocked on their neighbors' doors, asking for recyclable paper, metal, and rubber materials. They were proud to aid the war effort. They knew the items they collected—newspapers, toys, food cans, bike and car tires, garden hoses, cooking pots, rubber hot water bottles and beach balls, raincoats, nylon stockings, rags, and other household items—might be used to make tanks, ships, guns, ammunition, clothing, and other necessities for their brothers and fathers fighting in the war.

Children also used their own money to buy war bonds during bond drives held at school. The war bonds were savings bonds that the government sold to raise money for the war effort. But the bonds also helped to keep prices down: if people put their extra money into war bonds, they had less to spend on things. Kids bought war stamps, worth 10 cents each, which they pasted into books. When the book was complete, it could be traded in for a war bond.

At home, children helped their mothers bake cookies and cakes to send to the soldiers on the front lines. It was important that the troops knew America was supporting them. These packages were called "C mail" or cheer mail. Families also made patriotic banners called victory banners or sons-in-service flags to show their support for their sons, fathers, and brothers battling far away on the front lines. Banners were hung from a window or door at the front of the house where everyone could see them. The banners were white rectangles with a red border, and featured a blue star for every family member who was serving on the battlefront. If a soldier was killed, families would replace the blue star with a gold star.

★ WWII trivia ★

When Congress passed the Victory Tax, which taxed Americans on their income on a volunteer basis, the percentage of the U.S. population paying tax on their income increased from 3 to 62 percent! The U.S. government used Donald Duck in advertisements to persuade Americans to pay this volunteer income tax.

Make Your Own
Victory Banner

1 Cut the pillowcase in half so that you have one side of it. Cut this piece in half (you can make four victory banners out of one pillowcase).

2 Using the fabric glue attach a strip of ribbon to the bottom of your banner. Attach the opposite end, the top, to the wooden dowel. Make sure that the dowel extends an inch or so wider on each side.

3 Decide how wide you want your border to be. For example, you can have a border that is 1 inch wide all around, 2 inches wide all around, etc. Cut your red felt into strips of the same width and glue all the way around your banner.

4 Cut one or more stars out of the blue felt. Arrange and glue the blue felt stars in the center of the banner. If you want your stars to really sparkle, outline them in fabric glue and sprinkle with glitter. Over a piece of newspaper or your kitchen trashcan, hold your banner upright and gently shake it to remove the excess glitter.

5 To hang up your victory banner, tie the ends of a piece of ribbon or string to each end of the dowel. Leave enough slack in the ribbon so that it can loop over a hook.

Hang the victory banner on a window using a plastic suction cup hanger, or on your front door.

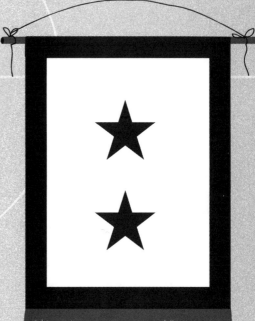

supplies

- ✪ old pillowcase or piece of white fabric
- ✪ scissors
- ✪ fabric glue
- ✪ beaded or fringed ribbon (gold, white, or blue)
- ✪ wooden dowel 2 inches wider than banner
- ✪ red and blue felt (optional: precut blue felt stars)
- ✪ red, gold, or blue glitter (optional)
- ✪ braided string or ribbon

Make Your Own
Papier-mâché Piggy Bank

During World War II kids saved their coins to buy war bonds. In this project, you're going to make a savings bank of your own.

1 Blow up a balloon to form the pig's body. Tie a knot. Cut a single cup from the egg carton and tape it to the end of the balloon for the pig's snout. Cut another cup in half and tape the halves to the balloon above the snout, forming the pig's ears.

2 Cut four more cups from the egg carton, and fashion legs for the pig. You may need to cut them down to size, depending on the size of the balloon. Keep the pig in proportion!

3 If you're using homemade papier-mâché, mix the flour and water in a large bowl. Tear the newspaper into narrow strips. Wet each strip thoroughly with the flour and water paste mixture, layering the newspaper strips all over the pig form in about four layers. This is very messy, but fun! If you're using the Celluclay, carefully apply it to the balloon without newspaper strips, just like clay.

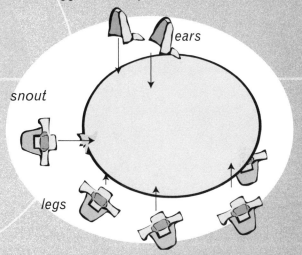

attach egg carton cups . . .

ears

snout

legs

supplies

✪ balloons

✪ egg carton

✪ scissors

✪ masking tape

✪ 3 cups flour and 6 cups warm water and newspaper

OR

✪ Celluclay instant papier-mâché paste (from a craft store)

✪ pipe cleaner

✪ paint (red, white, and blue)

✪ paint brush

✪ decorations: stickers, glitter, etc.

✪ spray varnish

apply papier-mâché

5 When your pig is dry, ask an adult to cut a coin slot in the top of the pig with a knife.

6 Decorate your pig with paint, stickers, even glitter. Use your imagination!

7 Ask your mom or dad to spray your bank with at least one coat of varnish to make it harder. Your piggy bank is ready to hold your coins!

4 Poke a curled-up pipe cleaner through the clay or newspaper. This is the pig's tail! Set your pig aside and let it dry for a couple of days.

paint after papier-mâché dries

⭐ **WWII trivia** ⭐

War bonds were popular Christmas presents during the war. Radio announcements encouraged people to loan the government 10 cents out of every dollar, promising that after the Allies won the war, Americans would have war bonds in their pockets instead of Axis bonds on their wrists.

FOOD
RATIONING

★ **During World War II, food was rationed for three primary reasons. One,** the military needed to send plenty of food to the soldiers fighting on the front lines. Two, access to products from other countries was cut off by the Axis enemies. And three, the ships that normally transported food were being used to send soldiers and military equipment to the battlefield. Remember, when there isn't enough of something that everyone wants, like gasoline or sugar, people who can afford to will pay more and more for it. The price will go up and up— that's inflation. Rationing keeps the price low and makes sure that everyone has equal access to the things they need. The government had tried voluntary rationing in World War I, but it didn't work very well, and inflation was very high. That meant that only people with lots of money could afford the basics. During World War II, people were told to watch their spending and to "Use it up, wear it out, make it do, or do without."

President Roosevelt knew he needed to come up with a ration program that would give people equal access to available food. So he created the Office of Price Administration (OPA) in 1941 and set up local war price and rationing boards that

★ WWII trivia ★

Jell-O Pudding was one of the few prepackaged foods available during the war, and was popular with American children. Other packaged foods included Spam, Ritz crackers, and Campbell's tomato soup.

gave out ration coupons. These local programs made sure that all Americans would have the same chance to buy rationed items, such as sugar, butter, meat, oils, processed baby foods, and canned or frozen fruits and vegetables.

The local ration boards were made up of area businesspeople and politicians. Board members came up with a ration level for each person or family in their program. How much a family was allowed depended on where they lived, who they worked for, and the number of people in their household. Each family member was issued a ration book that contained numbered stamp coupons. They had to turn in the coupons when they bought a rationed item. The stamps did not guarantee that food would always be available on store shelves, however.

Red meat was especially hard to get, and was a popular black market item. Remember, those who sold things on the black market operated illegally outside the government's ration system. Black marketers, known as "Mr. Black" or "Mr. B," sold their items for whatever price they could get, so prices could be quite high. Nylon stockings, for instance, sold for 20 times their pre-war price. The government fined store owners for participating in the black market if they were caught by one of the 3,100 OPA investigators.

Citizens were also fined for buying from black marketers. Many Americans thought it was unpatriotic to buy things on the black market. Other people thought it was a necessary evil of living through the war. What they forgot is that black marketers often took advantage of others who had the goods they wanted to sell, or had stolen what they were selling. Some cattle rustlers, for instance, snuck onto private ranches to steal cattle, which they quickly butch-

Dig for Victory

Before World War II started, Britain imported a lot of its food from other countries. Hitler, of course, ordered German battleships and submarines to hunt down and sink British ships carrying food and other supplies. The British government was eventually forced to set up a ration system. In the British system, shopkeepers were given just enough food for their registered customers. Some of the food that soon disappeared from British stores included oranges, lemons, bananas, and chocolate. To make sure people had fresh vegetables, the British government began a "Dig for Victory" campaign. It encouraged British families to grow their own vegetables. Over a million civilians did so, following the instructions of this rhyme:

"Dig! Dig! Dig! And your muscles will grow big
  Keep on pushing the spade
  Don't mind the worms
  Just ignore their squirms
  And when your back aches laugh with glee
  And keep on diggin'
  Til we give our foes a Wiggin'
  Dig! Dig! Dig! to Victory"

Many British citizens also kept chickens in their backyards, which provided them with eggs, and small livestock, such as rabbits, pigs, and goats.

ered and sold for lots of money.

To make sure that stores did not raise their prices too high, the OPA set a "ceiling," or top price, for each item sold in each store. Store owners had to post this price in plain sight. If shoppers noticed that stores were charging more than the ceiling price, they could turn to the OPA for help. Price ceilings helped to prevent inflation. The government also used advertising campaigns, targeted primarily to housewives, to urge Americans to comply with rations and avoid waste.

★ WWII trivia ★

When margarine was first manufactured, it wasn't colored so that it couldn't be confused with butter. Eventually, manufacturers included an orange food-coloring packet in the packaging. Children fought over who would get to open the packet and knead the color into the white block of margarine.

AM I PROUD!··

I'm fighting famine . . .
by canning food at home

⭐ **WWII trivia** ⭐

Bread was not rationed during the war, but the government decided that only whole, unsliced loaves could be sold, which would help keep the price of bread low. American cooks rushed to buy bread knives. That's where we get the phrase "the greatest thing since sliced bread."

Also, President Roosevelt created the National Wartime Nutrition Program, which reminded people that "Food is a weapon, don't waste it!" The government asked homemakers to only prepare what their families could eat in one sitting, although women certainly used up their leftovers in soups, sandwiches, and casseroles.

Posters with messages such as "Do with less, so they'll have enough!" were displayed in public to remind American citizens that rationing made sure that the Allied soldiers ate well. Other advertisements told homemakers to have "meatless days" during the week, to help reduce the demand for red meat. This was hard for many Americans—they were used to eating meat at dinner! Cooks also saved their waste kitchen fats. The glycerin in recycled fats could be used to make gunpowder and ammunition. Just one pound of fat contained enough glycerin to make a pound of black powder—enough for 50 bullets. Cooks took the fat to their butchers, who then turned it over to the government.

To make sure families had enough fresh fruits and vegetables, the government urged families to "Grow Your Own for Victory" by planting victory gardens in their backyards or in city plots. One reason the government wanted people to do this was to save the metal used to can fruits and vegetables. The military wanted to send its supplies of canned goods to the soldiers. Amazingly, Americans planted 20 million gardens! Soon, vegetables were sprouting up everywhere. In fact, victory gardens were so successful that they produced almost half of the vegetables that were eaten during the war in the United States. Some of

Women canning food at a community canning center.

the produce was even sent to help feed hungry Europeans, because their fields and crops were ruined by bombing raids.

America's victory gardens did cause one problem: How to keep the produce from spoiling? The answer: canning in glass jars. Many Americans had never canned food before, but they spent a lot of time canning their war crops. Sometimes it meant working far into the night after a long shift at a factory. People used pressure cookers, which use high heat and pressure, to make sure the glass canning jars were sealed properly. Pressure cookers became scarce due to demand, so many towns set up community canning centers. Some people also dried apples and other fruits. Some even rented locker space in frozen-food plant lockers to store their produce, but this could be inconvenient.

World War II cooks learned to find substitutes for rationed items. Two items that became quite hard to find were white sugar and butter. Yet cooks still wanted to serve desserts to their families. So instead of white sugar, they used molasses, brown sugar, honey, maple syrup, or corn syrup to sweeten cakes and cookies. They used margarine, vegetable shortening, or even the drippings from meat cooked at dinner if a recipe called for butter. Above all, American homemakers wanted to provide healthy meals for their families. The Food and Nutrition Board even gave out a chart of seven food groups to remind people that eating right would keep them healthy. "U.S. needs us strong," stated the chart, and "Eat the basic 7 every day." Fortunately, many items were never rationed during the war. These included eggs, soft cheeses, mayonnaise, dried fruits (prunes and raisins), fresh fish and shellfish, bread and cereals, fresh milk, dried pasta noodles, chicken, and jellies and preserves.

★ WWII trivia ★

The day after the bombing of Pearl Harbor, Americans hurried into stores to buy 100-pound bags of sugar. They knew, from the experience of the First World War, that sugar would soon be in short supply. Restaurants began putting less sugar in their sugar bowls, knowing that people were slipping the sugar cubes into their pockets before leaving the restaurant. When homemakers learned that the government planned to start rationing canned meat and fish, they rushed into stores with children's wagons, quickly emptying the shelves.

Make Your Own
Ration Cakes

1 Preheat oven to 325 degrees Fahrenheit. Line a cupcake tin with 12 paper cupcake holders.

2 With an adult's help, combine the honey, shortening, spices, salt, raisins, and water in a saucepan. Put on the stove and bring to a boil, stirring occasionally. Let mixture boil for 5 minutes. Remove from stove and cool.

3 In a bowl, thoroughly mix the flour, baking soda, and baking powder. For extra lightness, you can sift this mixture. Pour the cooled liquids into the flour mixture and stir everything together just until it's blended. Don't overstir. Pour batter into cupcake holders.

4 Bake for 20 minutes or until tops are brown. Let cool. Dust cupcakes with powdered sugar. Enjoy your butter-free, milk-free, egg-free, and white sugar-free spice cakes!

supplies

- ✪ cupcake papers
- ✪ ¾ cup honey
- ✪ 3 tablespoons shortening, such as **Crisco**
- ✪ 1 teaspoon ground cinnamon
- ✪ 1 teaspoon ground allspice
- ✪ ½ teaspoon salt
- ✪ 1 cup yellow raisins
- ✪ 1¼ cup water
- ✪ 2 cups all-purpose flour
- ✪ 1¼ teaspoon baking soda
- ✪ 1 teaspoon baking powder
- ✪ powdered sugar for dusting the tops of the cupcakes

Make Your Own
Tabletop Victory Garden

Plan to plant the seeds for your victory garden about six weeks before the last frost in your area, and then transplant the seedlings to a container or garden outdoors where they will get all the sunshine they need. If you plant herbs you can keep them indoors year round.

1 Place a layer of pea gravel in the bottom of your plastic tray. Add the seed-starting soil mix to each pot and position the pots in the tray. Add more gravel around each pot so each is secure.

2 Plant your seeds according to the directions on the packet. Label a Popsicle stick for each pot and stick it right in the soil by the rim of the pot. You'll have a lot of seeds left over. Share some with a friend or two!

LETTUCE SEEDS

Planting instructions on reverse.

3 Pick a counter or tabletop that will provide your garden with filtered (not direct) outdoor light for at least 5 or 6 hours a day. If your house doesn't get much light, you can help the plants with artificial light from a fluorescent lamp or a grow lamp.

BROCCOLI SEEDS

Planting instructions on reverse.

supplies

- ✪ pea gravel
- ✪ plastic tray with 2- or 3-inch-high sides
- ✪ several small plastic pots with holes in the bottom, one for each vegetable or herb you're going to plant (available in garden centers, or use leftover containers that your mom or dad might have from planting nursery-started flowers)
- ✪ sterile seed-starting soil mix
- ✪ seeds of your choice, perhaps tomato or bell pepper, lettuce, and herbs (such as chives, thyme, and basil)
- ✪ Popsicle sticks
- ✪ clear plastic bags with holes cut in them (one for each pot)
- ✪ spray bottle
- ✪ grow lamp (if your house doesn't get enough light)

★ WWII trivia ★

During World War II, the letter V could be seen all over America, in signs, on posters, and in fashion. Why? Because the V symbolized victory over America's enemies: Germany, Italy, and Japan.

4 Gently "flood" the gravel with water so that water is absorbed through the holes in the bottoms of the pots. This is better than pouring water directly into the pots. You can also mist the seeds using a spray bottle. Too much water will rot your seedling's new roots, so only water them enough to keep the soil slightly moist.

Schoolchildren work on a victory garden in 1943.

5 Cover the pots with the plastic bags so the soil stays warm and moist. The ideal temperature for growing plants from seed is 72 to 75 degrees Fahrenheit. Once they have sprouted, however, they will flourish in rooms with temperatures as low as 65 degrees. Make sure the plastic bags don't touch the plants once they start growing.

you remove it completely. You'll do the same thing before you transplant your seedlings outdoors. Let them spend some time outside every day for a week before you move them out permanently.

6 As soon as the seeds have sprouted a full set of leaves, remove the plastic bags so the plants don't overheat and die. Seedlings need good air circulation and light in order to grow strong. To avoid shocking the plants, however, take the plastic off for a couple of hours each day for a few days before

WORLD WAR II
FASHIONS

★ **American fashions changed a lot after the United States** entered the war. Before the war, American designers often copied the styles they observed on Paris fashion runways. Now they did not have access to European styles. Also, the War Production Board (WPB) set very strict guidelines on how much fabric, leather, and rubber could be used by the fashion industry. The WPB restricted American designers from using natural fabrics such as cotton and wool. They did this because the soldiers needed these materials for uniforms and blankets.

The WPB asked American designers to create styles that would stay in fashion throughout the war. Why? The WPB wanted to help American women feel that they could still be stylish. It's important to remember that in the 1940s, women ususally dressed up when they left their homes. They wore nylon stockings, hats or scarves, and gloves, and their hair was expected to be styled attractively. Popular hairstyles during the war included the Victory Roll and the Liberty Cut.

Just as homemakers found ways to be creative in the kitchen, designers looked for new ways to design clothes. They realized that rayon was one fabric they could find easily, after natural fibers were rationed. Rayon is made from wood pulp, and was first commercially manufactured in the United States in 1910. Because of

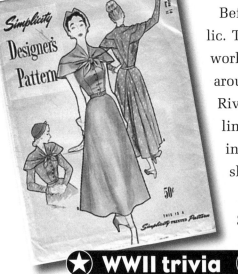

its texture, it was nicknamed "artificial silk." Designers liked rayon because it was comfortable to wear and could be easily dyed and blended with other fibers. When the WPB required women's dresses to be slimmer and shorter, with skirts only wide enough to allow women to sit and walk, designers raised hemlines to the knee and added buttons, to save zippers for the troops. They also removed pockets, because they required more material. During the war men's suits were made without cuffs or pleats.

Many women recycled outfits already hanging in their closets. They sewed new clothes using patterns from companies such as Simplicity, McCall, and Butterick. Homemakers used the patterns to turn their husband's old suits into new, tailored suits for themselves—and their old dresses into clothing for their children. Women and girls also made "dickeys," or detachable collars, which they wore under their sweaters. The dickeys made them look like they had many different blouses.

Before the war American women did not wear pants in public. They only wore them when they worked in the garden or lounged around the house. But Rosie the Riveter changed that! On assembly lines around the country, working women wore slack suits, and short-sleeved tops paired with pants or overalls.

"Mend and make new — to save buying new."

When tights and nylon hosiery became scarce, girls began wearing bobby socks. Many women applied makeup to their legs to make it look like they were wearing stockings. They used eyeliner pencil to draw seams up the back of their calves.

One of the hardest pieces of clothing to replace during the war was shoes. Both rubber and leather were rationed, so shoes were hard to buy. Often, family members pooled their shoe ration coupons to buy shoes for whomever needed them most. Even shoe heights were affected by the rations: women's heels could only be an inch and a half high. Some shoe designers got around the shortages by making shoe soles from cork!

Rubber shortages also meant that women stopped wearing rubber girdles, as they had before the war. What was a girdle? A tight rubber tube that a woman would wear around her waist and hips to give a trim look. Instead, women switched to wearing belts, which they buckled tightly around their waists. Women soon learned to appreciate the freedom from the uncomfortable girdle.

One thing women refused to give up, however, was the beauty shop. Beauty parlors offered women what they couldn't find elsewhere: pampering. Women enjoyed professional haircuts, facials, and manicures at beauty shops. Men, too, began using their barbershops for more than basic haircuts. There, men could listen to their favorite songs on the juke box and swap views about the latest war news.

During the war, even washing their clothes was a challenge for many Americans. For those who

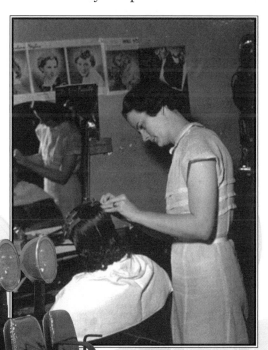

The beauty parlor.

WWII INVENTIONS

Nylon

Dr. Wallace H. Carothers was an employee of the DuPont Corporation when he invented nylon in 1938. DuPont decided to use it in manufacturing women's stockings, to compete with Japan's silk stockings. DuPont introduced nylon stockings at the 1939 New York World's Fair, but their popularity stalled when America entered World War II. The War Production Board restricted nylon to military use in parachutes and tires. However, when the war ended, women rushed to buy nylon stockings.

The bikini, influenced by the shortage of material during World War II, made its official debut in Paris pool fashion in 1946.

had a washing machine, it was a problem if the machine broke down. Once factories began making wartime products, they stopped making replacement parts for washing machines. Repairmen, too, were hard to find during the war. Some people washed their clothes by hand, but this took a lot of time and space. Others turned to laundries, although many laundries could not keep up with demand because workers often left for better-paying factory jobs. Many laundry owners were forced to turn away customers.

When the war ended in 1945, Americans were quick to buy new fashions made with yards and yards of material. Women mobbed stores and waited in long lines for their beloved nylon stockings. In fact, until the DuPont company was able to crank up its hosiery production, American women across the country got into fights with each other when stores ran out of stock. Don't believe it? Then consider this: the mayor of Pittsburgh arranged for a stocking sale in response to a petition by 400 women. On the day of the sale, 40,000 people lined up to fight for 13,000 pairs! America breathed a sigh of relief when DuPont began producing 30 million pairs a month in 1946, putting an end to the "Nylon Riots."

Step into
Rosie's Shoes

In this activity you're going to become Rosie the Riveter by making your own kerchief from a bandana, donning a short-sleeved blue shirt, and striking the famous Rosie pose. Grab the Polaroid camera and make your own Rosie the Riveter poster!

1 Use your pencil to sketch the words of the Rosie the Riveter poster onto the top of your yellow poster board. Use the white paint for the words, and the blue paint to fill in around the words, copying the style of the poster. Add a blue strip of paint to the bottom of the poster as well. Using your white gel pen be sure to credit the "War Production Co-Ordinating Committee."

2 Allow the poster to dry, then hang it on your wall or on a bulletin board. It needs to be positioned high enough so that the words are just above your head when you stand in front of it. See the original poster for placement.

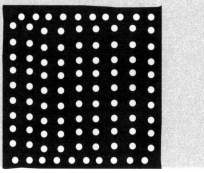
bandana

supplies

- ✪ large piece of yellow poster board or art paper, a few inches taller than you are from your waist to the top of your head and a few inches wider than you are when striking the Rosie pose
- ✪ pencil
- ✪ blue and white paint
- ✪ 2 large paint brushes
- ✪ white gel pen
- ✪ large red bandana or a piece of cloth, red with white polka dots if possible
- ✪ blue shirt
- ✪ mirror (optional)

3 Fold the bandana or cloth in half to form a triangle. Place the long side of the triangle at the base of your hairline along your neck, holding one of the pointed ends in each hand. Tie a knot on the top of your head, making sure the bandana fits snugly around your head. Bring the free tip of the triangle up over your head, securing the tip firmly under the knot.

fold bandana

place bandana behind your head and bring corners up

4 Put on a blue shirt—roll up the sleeves if it's long-sleeved.

5 Stand sideways in front of the poster, set your face in determination, and strike the famous Rosie pose. It's time for your photo op! Have someone hold up a mirror, if you like, so you can adjust your pose until you're happy with it. Then have your picture taken so that the poster (with you in it) fills the frame.

tie corners

tuck third corner under knot

★ WWII trivia ★

When the United States needed to expand its workforce during World War II, the idea of women working in factories was completely new. Many women (and men) did not feel comfortable with this idea. The government used propaganda to change public opinion, to convince Americans that it was the patriotic duty of women to work where the country most needed them. The propaganda used Rosie the Riveter as its symbol. Rosie wasn't a specific person, she *represented* all women who worked. The campaign was so successful that Rosie the Riveter became the symbol for working women both during the war and after it ended. Rosie the Riveter has even been credited with making it acceptable for women to wear pants.

In 2000, Rosie the Riveter Memorial and National Historical Park officially opened in Richmond, California, at a shipyard where many women worked during the war. There is even a web site devoted to her: www.rosietheriveter.com!

Make Your Own
Victory Pin

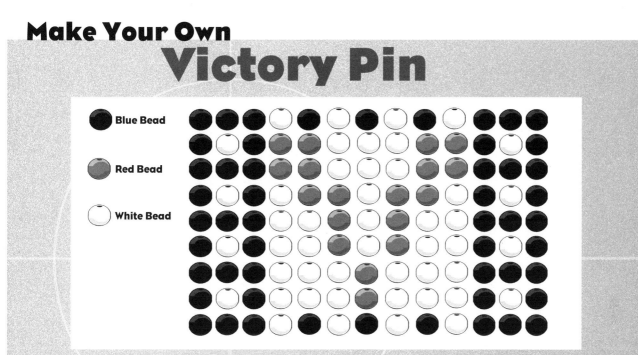

Blue Bead

Red Bead

White Bead

The chart shows how the beads should be placed on the small safety pins. Each safety pin will represent one column.

1 Open one small safety pin, add the seed beads for column one, which are all blue, and close. Pinch the end of the safety pin with the pliers so it won't pop open later. Repeat for the remaining rows, following the pattern on the chart. Keep the safety pins in order as you finish them.

2 Take the large safety pin and open it. Use the flat-head screwdriver to slightly pry the coils at the end apart.

3 Thread the small beaded pins onto the larger pin, starting with the first column one. Do this by slipping the loop of the small beaded safety pin onto the large pin. Pull the small pin down to the loop at the base of the large pin. Pull it around the loop and up the back-side of the pin. Do this with all of the pins, being careful to keep them in order.

4 When you've added all of the small pins, use the pliers to squeeze the loop closed. This will keep the small pins from sliding off. Wear your *V for Victory* pin proudly!

supplies

- ✪ **13 safety pins, each 1¹⁄₁₆ inches long**
- ✪ **1 safety pin, 2 inches long**
- ✪ **seed beads in red, white, and blue**
- ✪ **needle-nose pliers**
- ✪ **flat-head screwdriver**

WAR-TIME FUN

★ **Even though there was a war going on, Americans still wanted to have** fun. Although Congress passed a 5 percent "Victory Tax" in 1942 to help fund the war, American civilians didn't hesitate to spend their money on fun. And why not? Most people had purchased plenty of savings and war bonds (more than $140 billion by 1945), they were working hard for victory, and there were few luxury items to buy except on the black market.

So, folks plunked down their extra dollars at the horse tracks and nightclubs. They filled movie theaters, roller rinks, bowling alleys, restaurants, and places featuring live bands or juke boxes. And in United Service Organization (USO) centers around the country, soldiers found steaming cups of coffee and local girls happy to join them in the lively dance called the Lindy Hop. Others glided their dance partners through the fox-trot, serenaded by the soothing tunes of big-band music. President Roosevelt established the

New Year's Eve dance iat the USO club in Philadelphia.

★ WWII trivia ★

The USO sponsored more than 400,000 shows for U.S. troops between 1941 and 1947. USO canteens in towns across the United States offered food, fun, and entertainment to soldiers on leave.

Know Your Swing Slang

killer-diller: good stuff
snap your cap: get angry
licorice stick: clarinet
threads: clothing

USO program so that soldiers home on leave would have welcoming places where they could go for a break from the stress of war. The president asked civilians to donate the funds to run these centers.

At home, families listened to their living room radios for fun. Children sat spellbound, caught up in the exciting adventures of *The Lone Ranger*, *Amos 'n' Andy*, and *Superman*. Throughout the war, radio programming was rich with dramas, comedies, action-adventure programs, soap operas, and children's shows. These entertaining programs were often broadcast in front of live studio audiences.

THE USO

In 1940, President Franklin Roosevelt realized that American soldiers were in need of an organized recreation program when they were on leave. So he asked six private organizations to band together to pool their resources and form the **United Service Organizations**, known as the USO. These six groups were the YMCA (Young Men's Christian Association), YWCA (Young Women's Christian Association), National Catholic Community Service, the National Jewish Welfare Board, the Traveler's Aid Association, and the Salvation Army. The USO was officially launched in New York state on February 4, 1941. That year movie stars and other celebrities began to participate in "Camp Shows" at U.S. military bases. They did so without getting paid, knowing it was one way they could show the troops how important they were in the fight for victory. When U.S. troops began serving overseas, the entertainers traveled there as well. By 1944, USO centers were operating in more than 3,000 locations across the country, in churches, museums, barns, beach clubs, stores, mansions, and railroad sleeping cars. There, GIs found a "home away from home," a place to relax, watch movies, write letters, laugh at the jokes of professional entertainers, and dance with the local girls.

War-Time Celebrities

Musicians: Glenn Miller, the Ink Spots, Frank Sinatra, the Andrews Sisters, Jimmy Dorsey, Perry Como

Entertainers: Lucille Ball, Red Skelton, Bob Hope, Milton Berle, Jack Benny

Comic characters: Joe Palooka, Blondie, Li'l Abner, Little Orphan Annie, Dick Tracy, Gasoline Alley

Families also enjoyed playing chess, checkers, and card games. Despite paper shortages, book sales soared. Teenagers even got their own magazine in 1944, with the launch of *Seventeen*. Teens spent a lot of time dancing and playing pool in teen centers across the country. Many centers opened primarily to keep the kids out of mischief. Some parents were simply working too many hours—or off fighting the war—to monitor their kids' behavior as much as they wanted to.

★ WWII trivia ★

Teenagers became a recognized economic group during World War II. Many teenagers had part-time jobs that gave them plenty of cash—and little to spend it on. Advertisers began aiming ads at teens, hoping they would buy their products after the war.

WWII INVENTIONS

GI Joe Comic Strip

American comic artist David Berger introduced the world to the term "GI Joe" (Government Issue Joe) with his comic strip. The comic strip debuted on June 17, 1942, in the military's *YANK* magazine and *Stars and Stripes* newspaper. Berger served in the army during World War II.

Everyone went to their nearby movie theaters. A double feature cost only about 25 cents and popcorn was a dime more. A trip to the movies could last up to six hours, if someone stayed for the news reel, cartoon, serial western, and the feature film. *The Three Stooges* and *Abbott and Costello* were two of Hollywood's most popular comedy teams.

Ninety million people went to the movies each week. President Roosevelt believed movies were an effective way to inform and entertain citizens. But it

Gasoline Rations

During the war, the Japanese seized plantations in the Dutch East Indies (what is now Indonesia) that produced 90 percent of America's raw rubber. Gasoline and rubber rationing caused the greatest inconvenience to American civilians. When gas rationing went into effect on December 1, 1942, each motorist was assigned a windshield sticker with a letter A, B, or C for their car, or a T sticker for their truck. The T sticker allowed truckers unlimited gas, but many drivers received the lowly A sticker, which allowed them to buy only 3 or 4 gallons of gasoline each week. People who worked in factories and drove car pools often received the green B sticker, which allowed them about 8 gallons of gasoline each week. Doctors were given the more generous red C sticker, while congressmen and other VIPs (Very Important People) received the rare X sticker. When gas was rationed, department stores stopped making deliveries to their customers, and milk deliveries were reduced to every other day. The Office of Price Administration even banned civilians from "pleasure driving" and sometimes fined people they caught driving to restaurants, the horse racetrack, athletic stadiums, or the symphony. Soon, people were piling onto overcrowded trains when they wanted to get to other cities. The rationing of gasoline and rubber made many travelers turn to the black market.

was hard to make movies during the war years. Hollywood made more than a thousand movies during the war, but movie companies had to deal with lots of shortages. Film was in short supply. So were nails: they had to be removed from old movie sets to build new ones. Razor blades, which the filmmakers used to cut and edit the films, were hard to find. And Hollywood's stunt windows, made from sugar so that they would easily break when an actor crashed through them, could

★ WWII trivia ★

Dancing was so popular during the war that more than 2,000 war plants offered on-site areas where workers could dance during their breaks and lunch.

★ WWII trivia ★

Baseball was very popular during the war. When 4,000 of the 5,700 players in the major and minor leagues enlisted in the military, older or disabled players took their spots, as did players from Cuba and Mexico. The All American Girls Professional Baseball League (AAGPBL), established in 1943, also drew thousands of cheering fans. Young girls who dreamed of playing had to join a junior league first. They had to be at least 12 and ready to play every Tuesday and Saturday. When the war ended, the girl's league struggled when the men's major league games resumed. By 1954, it ended because of lack of interest.

no longer be made when sugar became rationed. Even the legendary searchlights, which Hollywood usually flashed across the skies during movie premiers, were darkened. And, of course, Hollywood lost many of its most popular actors when they volunteered or were drafted to fight.

Some forms of entertainment were closed when they weren't careful to follow government's guidelines. For instance, horseracing became quite popular during the war, and millions of Americans bet on their favorite steeds. But the government shut down the tracks in 1945. Why? The official reason was that racetracks were not important to the war effort. But many thought the real reason was government officials were upset that civilians were disregarding the government's ban on leisure driving. Others believed it was because track owners refused to hold war bond drives. When the tracks shut down, many horse owners had to sell or kill their horses because of the high costs of maintaining them. Other owners simply shipped their horses to Mexico City, to compete in races there.

Make Your Own
Silly Putty™

During World War II, Japan invaded numerous rubber-producing countries, cutting the United States off from the rubber supplies it needed to manufacture truck tires and boots. So the War Production Board asked American companies to develop a synthetic rubber. James Wright, a General Electric engineer, invented a gooey, bouncy substance when he combined boric acid and silicone oil in a test tube. Wright didn't see a use for it, but marketing whiz Peter Hodgson thought it would make a great toy. He was right. When Hodgson introduced it to American kids in 1949 it was an instant hit. In 2000, Silly Putty celebrated its 50th year of popularity and it was inducted into the National Toy Hall of Fame.

What's that word that means making a discovery that was not sought after? Serendipity! While the creation of Silly Putty was certainly serendipitous, millions of kids around the world now have the thrill of playing with it. It bounces! It picks up newsprint images! And best of all—it's something you can make in your own kitchen!

1 Pour the glue and liquid starch into the baggie. This is easier to do if you set the baggie into a small bowl.

2 Lock the baggie. Carefully squish the contents together until they're well mixed. Make sure you don't apply too much pressure, or the top of the bag might open!

3 When well mixed, add the food coloring of your choice. You can make separate batches in different colors.

4 To keep your Silly Putty from drying out, place it in a baggie when you're not playing with it.

supplies

- 2 cups Elmer's all-purpose glue
- 1 cup liquid starch (available in grocery stores)
- large zip-lock baggies
- 3 drops of food coloring—you pick the color!

Make Your Own
Animation Flip Book

So, you're a kid in World War II, and you've donated your favorite metal toys to scrap drives. What are you gonna do for fun? Make your own, of course! In this project, you'll make your own animation flip book using only your imagination, a pencil, and some paper. When you flip the pages really fast, guess what? You've got an instant cartoon!

1 Decide what object you would like to animate. Perhaps a plane flying across a cloudy sky or two boys bouncing a ball? On some scrap paper, draw the first and last pictures of your scene. Use these as your guides to remember what action your object(s) will complete.

2 Turn the small pad sideways, so the bound side is on the left. You will hold this side as you flip the pages with your right thumb. Note that you won't be able to see the left-hand side of your drawings as well when you're holding it, so keep the main action on the right two-thirds.

3 Start drawing on the last page

of your notebook or Post-it pad. Draw the last scene of your action. If it is the plane, then perhaps draw just the tail of the plane peeking through a cloud. If it is the boys, then perhaps draw one boy holding the ball.

4 Flip the next page down and draw the next scene. Draw the scene as it would look just a moment before the scene that follows it. You'll be able to see the previous page through the paper, which will help guide you.

5 When you're done with your pages, go back and fill in detail, or remove any pages that you don't like. Leave two blank sheets on top of the flip book.

6 On the top page draw a cover for your flip-book movie. On the second page, put your name. Reinforce the bound side of the paper by adding strips of clear tape. This will make sure the pages stay together.

7 Flip through the book really fast to watch your movie.

supplies

- ✪ **3-by-5-inch pad of white paper**
  OR
- ✪ **a rectangular pad of Post-it notes**
- ✪ **pencil**
- ✪ **clear tape**

PRISONS OF DISCRIMINATION

★ **When Japanese pilots bombed Pearl Harbor in Hawaii, on December 7,** 1941, the lives of all Americans were changed when America declared war on Japan. One group of Americans were affected by the bombing in ways different from others: Japanese Americans who lived on the West Coast of the United States. These Japanese Americans were forced to leave their homes, board trains, and move to isolated prison camps.

On the day Pearl Harbor was bombed, about 126,000 **first-generation** Japanese Americans (called "Issei") and their children (called "Nisei"), were living in the United States. Many of them had been in America for more than 20 years. A census taken in 1940 showed that 62 percent of Japanese Americans had been born in the United States. This fact meant that these people should have had the full rights of citizenship. The census also showed that more than 157,000 Japanese Americans were living in Hawaii.

Though their children were citizens, the Issei were classified as aliens. All Asians born outside of the United States were not allowed to become American citizens. Laws were passed in the 1920s against it. Because they felt unwelcome, many of these residents lived apart from American society and kept to themselves. This did little to

AVENGE
December 7

U.S. Internment and POW Camps

Most people in the United States know that more than 120,000 Japanese Americans in California were sent to internment camps in isolated areas of the West during World War II. It is less well known that German and Italian Americans who had lived in the United States for years were also rounded up and held in internment camps. Even people from Germany and Austria who lived in South and Central America were sent to the United States and interned.

The United States was also home to dozens of prisoner-of-war (POW) camps. Hundreds of thousands of German and Italian soldiers were sent from the battlefields of North Africa and Europe to camps in the United States, where they spent the rest of the war far from the fighting. Most POWs worked on farms or did manual labor. When the war was over, these POWs were shipped back to their home countries to help rebuild Europe.

Japanese Americans at the train station to be moved to internment camps.

build understanding and acceptance. By working hard, however, many Japanese Americans flourished and built up successful small businesses, proving themselves worthy members of the United States.

Japanese Americans considered America their home, and they were just as horrified and angered by Japan's attack on Pearl Harbor as any other American was. Sadly, many Americans were unwilling to look beyond their Asian features. When the FBI began searching Japanese American homes for hidden radio equipment—without warrants—the Japanese Americans realized that they did not have any rights. And when 7,000 Japanese men were arrested and sent to special prisons, just in case they were spies, there was nothing they could do.

Some individual Americans—and businesses—demanded that Japanese residents be sent back to Japan. It is important to understand that in the first few weeks after the Pearl Harbor attack, Japanese Americans, as a group, were not considered a threat. But the attack on Pearl Harbor gave people who were jealous of the success of many Japanese Americans the opportunity to get rid of them. Japanese farmers were producing nearly 40 percent of California's crops and there were many who were happy to take that from them.

People began to spread rumors about the Japanese Americans. One rumor was that Japanese farmers were forming arrow shapes in their fields to direct Japanese bombers to U.S. targets. Even the *San Francisco Chronicle* began to print stories designed to cause hysteria. Soon, fearful residents of the Western states demanded that Japanese Americans be rounded up and sent away. Even California's attorney general, Earl Warren, and representatives to Congress began to pressure Washington legislators to remove the "Japs." To protect themselves from persecution, Chinese residents wore buttons that read "I'm Chinese" and "I hate the Japs as much as you do."

At first the government only imposed **curfews** on Japanese Americans. They couldn't travel more than 5 miles from their homes, and had to be in their homes after 9 p.m. They also couldn't go near military bases, power plants, or boat docks—and if they worked at such a place they were fired. But on February 19, 1942, President Roosevelt signed Executive Order 9066, which gave the military the authority to relocate all Japanese Americans living on the West Coast. Families were given only one week to sell their homes and businesses, find homes for their pets, and pack a few belongings. Japanese Americans living in Hawaii, however, did not have to go to camps. Nearly half of the population in Hawaii was of Japanese descent, so the government decided it was not practical to try to intern them.

With the order in effect, the government realized it had a huge problem on its hands. Public sentiment against the Japanese was high and states outside

I'M CHINESE

JAPS CH AS YOU DO

WESTERN DEFENSE COMMAND AND FOURTH ARMY WARTIME CIVIL CONTROL ADMINISTRATION
Presidio of San Francisco, California
May 23, 1942

INSTRUCTIONS TO ALL PERSONS OF JAPANESE ANCESTRY
Living in the Following Area:

Internment notice.

STOP
AREA LIMITS
FOR PERSONS OF JAPANESE ANCESTRY RESIDING IN THIS RELOCATION CENTER
SENTRY ON DUTY

Know Your WWII Words

first-generation: people who live in the United States but were born in another country

curfew: a time when people have to be off the streets

Japanese American boys stand at the fence of their internment camp.

of California refused to allow Japanese Americans to move in. What would it do with the Japanese Americans living on the West Coast? President Roosevelt set up the War Relocation Authority (WRA), which quickly built nine camps in isolated areas of Idaho, Wyoming, Arizona, and Oklahoma to house the Japanese for the rest of the war. These states had low populations compared to other states in the country. This relocation of Japanese Americans was the largest single forced evacuation in American history.

When the Japanese Americans arrived at their new homes, they noticed the gun-toting guards, the poor construction, the lack of furnishings, and the crowded conditions. They quickly built their own tables and chairs, planted their own gardens and trees, and added screens to the public toilets to offer a small amount of privacy. Children went to school, but they didn't have the books, laboratory equipment, and sporting equipment that other American children had. Peering through the barbed-wire fences that imprisoned them, the Japanese Americans must have wondered if they would be allowed to stay in America, and longed to return to their homes and businesses.

In 1943, after the U.S. government overturned its ban on Nisei enlisting in the military, army recruiters visited the camps and offered the prisoners a way out: the Japanese American citizens could prove their loyalty to the United States by enlisting in the military. Many of the internees were angered by this, but some chose to enlist rather than stay in the camps.

In 1944, all Japanese American prisoners were allowed to leave the camps, when the U.S. Supreme Court ruled that the forced internment violated U.S. constitutional principles. Many of the residents struck out for a brighter future, moving to Cincinnati, St. Louis, Chicago, New York, New Jersey, and Philadelphia. Over 90,000 internees eventually returned to California to rebuild their lives. The U.S. government agreed, under the Japanese American Evacuation Claims Act of 1948, to pay those who had lived in the camps for their property losses. In 1988, Congress passed House Resolution 442, which awarded an apology and $20,000 to every internee.

Make Your Own
Paper Crane

There is an old Japanese legend that anyone who folds 1,000 paper cranes will be granted a wish. Paper cranes are made using the Japanese art of paper folding called origami. People from all over the world send paper cranes to a monument in Hiroshima Peace Park dedicated to the victims of the atomic bombings in Japan. You can learn more about the monument and the girl that inspired it on this web site: www.sadako.com.

1 All you need is a 6-inch square piece of paper. Place the colored side face up on the table. Fold diagonally to form a triangle. Be sure the points line up. Make all creases very sharp. Unfold the paper. Now fold the paper diagonally in the opposite direction, forming a new triangle.

2 Unfold the paper and turn it over so the white side is up. The dotted lines in the diagram are creases you have already made. Fold the paper in half to the right to form a rect-angle. Unfold the paper. Fold the paper in half to the top to form a new rectangle.

3 Unfold the rectangle, but don't flatten it out. Your paper will have the creases shown by the dotted lines in the figure. Bring all four corners of the paper together, folding the paper into the flat square shown on the right. This square has an open end where all four corners of the paper come together. It also has two flaps on the right and two flaps on the left.

4 Lift the upper right flap, and fold in the direction of the arrow. Crease along line a-c. Lift the upper left flap and fold in the direction of the arrow. Crease along the line a-b. Lift the paper at point d and fold down the triangle bdc. Crease along the line b-c. Undo the three folds you just made and your paper will have the crease lines shown.

5 Lift just the top layer of the paper at point a. Think of this as opening a frog's mouth. Open it up and back to line b-c. Crease the line b-c inside the frog's mouth. Press

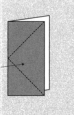

on points b and c to reverse the folds along lines a-b and a-c. The trick is to get the paper to lie flat in the long diamond shape shown here. At first it will seem impossible. Have patience.

6 Turn the paper over. Repeat steps 4 and 5 on this side. Your paper will look like this diamond with two "legs" at the bottom. Taper the diamond at its legs by folding the top layer of each side in the direction of the arrows along lines a-f and a-e so that they meet at the center line. Flip the paper over and repeat on this side to complete the tapering of the two legs.

7 This figure has two skinny legs. Lift the upper flap at point f (be sure it's just the upper flap), and fold it over in the direction of the arrow as if turning the page of a book. This is called a "book fold." Flip the entire figure over. Repeat this book fold on this side. Be sure to fold over only the top "page."

8 This figure looks like a fox with two pointy ears at the top and a pointy nose at the bottom. Open the upper layer of the fox's mouth at point a, and crease it along line g-h so the fox's nose touches the top of the fox's ears. Turn the figure over and repeat so that all four points touch.

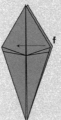

9 Now for another book fold. Lift the top layer (at point f), and fold it in the direction of the arrow. Flip the entire figure over. Repeat the book fold on this side.

10 There are two points, a and b, below the upper flap. Pull out each one, in the direction of the arrows, as far as shown. Press down along the base (at points x and y) to make them stay in place. Take the end of one of the points, and bend it down to make the head of the crane. Using your thumbnail, reverse the crease in the head, and pinch it to form the beak. The other point becomes the tail. Open the body by blowing into the hole underneath the crane, and gently pulling out the wings.

ON THE
FRONT LINES

★ **When the leaders of a country decide to go to war, they have to think** very carefully about many things: how many people will be killed, how much money it will cost, how many sacrifices people must make, and whether or not the war can be won. When war broke out in Europe in 1939, many people in the United States did not want the country to go to war. They had fought a war only 20 years before, and the war in Europe seemed very far away. Congressmen tried to convince President Roosevelt that the war was none of the United States' business. But many Americans watched the Nazis devouring large sections of Europe. They expressed their willingness to fight for democracy if their president asked them to do so.

When Japan bombed Pearl Harbor, the war suddenly became very personal for all Americans. People across the country united to stop Japan, as well as the other Axis powers. Many men—and women—volunteered for military service as soon as

Kilroy Was Here

During World War II, the words "Kilroy Was Here!" began to appear as graffiti at home and wherever the U.S. military traveled abroad. Eventually the phrase, and the cartoon character that often accompanied it, came to represent America's worldwide presence. But who started the art craze? In 1946 the Transit Company of America held a contest to find out. It offered the prize of a trolley car to the serviceman who could prove he was the real Kilroy. Almost 40 men stepped forward to make that claim, but James Kilroy, a shipyard inspector during the war, brought along officials from the shipyard and some of the riveters to help prove his authenticity. James Kilroy won the trolley car, gave it to his nine children as a Christmas gift, and set it up in their front yard as a playhouse.

"THE GIRL HE LEFT BEHIND" IS STILL BEHIND HIM She's a WOW

Roosevelt declared war on December 8, 1941. Barred from fighting on the front lines, women still played a critical role in the fight against Germany, Japan, and Italy. As nurses and transport pilots, journalists and photographers, they willingly entered battle zones to save lives, ferry soldiers and supplies, and record the war.

Yet, many of the men and women who helped the Allies to win the war did not spend time in military cockpits or hospitals. Some slipped deep behind enemy lines to serve as spies. Others worked in government offices and secret laboratories, racing against time to break Axis message codes in order to monitor military messages and troop movements. Scientists, too, made huge contributions, using their skills to develop and refine new technologies, such as **radar** and **sonar**, which gave the Allies a strong advantage over Hitler. Some scientists even figured out how to contain—and unleash—the fury of **atomic energy** in the building of **atomic bombs**. Engineers invented new weapons that helped the Allies

The Star-Spangled Banner

O say, can you see, by the dawn's early light,
What so proudly we hail'd at the twilight's last gleaming?
Whose broad stripes and bright stars, thro' the perilous fight,
O'er the ramparts we watch'd, were so gallantly streaming?
And the rockets' red glare, the bombs bursting in air,
Gave proof thro' the night that our flag was still there.
O say, does that star-spangled banner yet wave
O'er the land of the free and the home of the brave?

The first verse of the song written by Francis Scott Key on Sept. 13, 1814, during the War of 1812. It wasn't officially adopted as the national anthem of the United States until 1931.

to gain a footing on enemy territory, including **amphibious** trucks that operated as well in water as they did on land. Incendiary (fire) bombs destroyed buildings. Even the way war was conducted changed during World War II, with military strategists using bomb raids that "carpeted" cities with thousands of tons of dropped bombs.

Despite all this support, it quickly became obvious that more American soldiers were needed on the front lines. President Roosevelt had signed the Selective Training and Service Act, known as the draft, into law on September 16, 1940, more than a year before the United States entered the war. The draft required men

American bombers attack a vital aircraft engine repair depot in Nazi-occupied Paris, France, 1943.

Know Your WWII Words

radar: a system for locating an object with radio signals

sonar: a device that detects the presence and location of an object under water, like a submarine, using sonic and ultrasonic waves that reflect off the object

atomic energy: energy released by changes in the nucleus of an atom

atomic bomb: a bomb with explosive power from the release of atomic energy

amphibious: belonging or working on both land and water

casualties: people killed, wounded, captured, or missing in action in a war

between the ages of 21 and 30 to sign up for military service, whether they wanted to serve or not. Later, the draft was extended to men ages 18 to 45. Between 1940 and 1944, U.S. troop strength swelled from 50,000 to 12 million. Some of the U.S. troops that fought the hardest were African Americans and Japanese Americans who saw the war as an opportunity to prove their value to American society.

By the end of the war, many American soldiers, sailors, and pilots had been wounded or killed. Those who die or are wounded in a war are called **casualties**. The United States lost more than 400,000 military members and about 6,000 civilians. Overall, nearly 60 million people from around the world lost their lives in this truly global war, making it the bloodiest conflict the world has yet experienced. The Soviet Union lost 28 million people, more than any other nation, but millions died in many other countries, including Germany, with nearly million (more than half of which were Jews and civilians).

"above and beyond the call of duty"

DORIE MILLER
Received the Navy Cross
at Pearl Harbor, May 27, 1942

8

With all that loss of life, were the U.S. legislators who hoped to keep the United States out of the war right? Could America have stayed neutral—and still remained the "land of the free and the home of the brave?" Perhaps. But without the United States joining the fight with Britain and the Soviet Union against Germany, Italy, and Japan, the Axis powers might have won the war, and the world would be a very different place.

United States
400,000 servicemen died
6,000 civilians lost

Soviet Union
lost 28 million people

Great Britain
almost 500,000 dead

China
more than 17 million dead

Germany
nearly 8 million people died

Poland
lost almost 6 million

World Wide
nearly 60 million
people died

SPYING
FOR SECRETS

During the war, both the Axis and Allies relied on military intelligence to figure out what the enemy was up to. Where, for instance, were the Japanese sending their planes and ships? How many tank divisions did the German Army have in France? And how could the Allies best confuse Hitler and his generals to give the invasion of Normandy (D-day) the greatest chance of success? The information couldn't come from spy satellites, because they didn't exist yet. Important sources of information were **surveillance**, codebreaking, and signals interception.

Intelligence organizations trained groups of men and women to gather the information in person, which is called reconnaissance. These spies slipped behind enemy lines, often by parachute, knowing that they could be captured or killed. Their plan was simple: steal information, persuade enemy residents to hand over information, and spread false information when and where they could. Some of the agents even trained as **saboteurs**, becoming experts at setting explosives. To create chaos or confusion in Axis areas, they sometimes cut phone and power wires, destroyed equipment, blasted bridges and tunnels, and tried to get local residents to panic or

LISTEN...

SOMEONE TOLD ME...

AND I SAW...

I HEAR THAT...

DO YOU KNOW...

I KNOW THAT...

U-BOAT CAPTAIN KILLS 22 SAILORS

Laughs as He Torpedoes
Lifeboat Leaving Doom-
ed Vessel.

RUMORS COST US LIVES

British Spitfire

A deck of playing cards could conceal a map to safety.

riot. They did what they could to help the local **resistance**.

But not all reconnaissance was done on the ground. Aerial reconnaissance relied on small, fast, high-flying aircraft, such as the British Spitfire, to take photographs of enemy troop movements. Unlike the clumsy, low-flying bomber planes used in World War I, these single-seat fighter planes could fly at higher altitudes, which helped them to go undetected. But just in case ground spotters were on the lookout, the planes were painted in **camouflage** colors to blend in with the sky.

The United States gathered some of its intelligence through an organization established on June 13, 1942, called the Office of Strategic Services (OSS). The OSS director was William J. "Wild Bill" Donovan, a Medal of Honor recipient who had fought the Germans in World War I. At its peak in 1944, the OSS team included 13,000 men and women. Most OSS recruits were under the age of 30, held college degrees, and could speak a foreign language. After the war the OSS eventually became the Central Intelligence Agency (CIA), which remains in operation today.

OSS engineers and technicians also produced some of the best spy equipment used by the Allies against the Axis foes. Because camouflage and secrecy were the two things

Fooled You!

Juan Pujol Garcia was an effective British counterintelligence agent during World War II. Although he was working for the British, he was able to convince the Germans that he was spying for them. Under his code name, Garbo, Garcia gave fake intelligence to Germany in hundreds of radio transmissions. He pretended to have more than 20 agents working for him! Garcia helped to persuade the Germans that the Allies' D-day landing was a **decoy** for a larger invasion elsewhere on the French coast. This greatly aided the success of the Allied invasion of Europe.

Know Your WWII Words

surveillance: to observe or watch someone

intelligence: information about an enemy

sabotage: causing problems for the enemy, like blowing up bridges or destroying a pipeline

saboteur: someone who tries to cause problems for the enemy

the Resistance: an organized movement in a conquered country to sabotage the invaders

camouflage: a disguise that makes something look like its background so you can't see it very well

microfilm: a narrow strip of film with very small pictures on it so a lot of information can be stored in a small space

microdot: a photograph the size of a dot so it can be moved secretly

decoy: a fake that tricks someone into going in the wrong direction

guerrilla warfare: military action by small groups that harass the enemy, interrupt lines of communication, and destroy supplies

espionage: spying

OSS agents needed to stay alive, they were given special tools, such as hidden radios, cameras, and maps. OSS technicians rigged cans of talcum powder and shaving cream with hollow sections that could be used to hide film containers. They also invented cameras small enough to fit on a wristwatch, and hollowed out real coins so the agents and spies could use them to hide **microfilm** and **microdots**. The British had nifty spy tools, too. Some British agents, for example, attached fake rubber soles to their boots before they landed on Japanese-occupied beaches. The rubber soles were shaped like human feet, so their footprints blended in with those of local residents—who generally went barefoot. Pretty clever, huh?!

The OSS had its own spy branch called the SI, or Secret Intelligence branch, that operated in Europe, Asia, and the Middle East. It secretly placed nearly 200 volunteer spies (Axis prisoners of war who had been in prison in Britain) into the Nazi

Spy Acronyms & Names

OSS: (Office of Strategic Services) The American spy agency that evolved into the CIA (Central Intelligence Agency)

SOE: (Special Operations Executive) British spy agency focusing on espionage and sabotage

SIS: (Secret Intelligence Service) British spy agency focusing on espionage and sabotage

MI9: British spy agency that developed tools for its spies

Abwehr: German spy agency

SD: (Sicherheitsdienst or Security Service) German spy agency that used agents to gather information about anti-Nazi and other activity throughout Europe and the rest of the world

Gestapo: (Geheime Staatspolizei or Secret State Police) German secret police force known for torture and violence used by Hitler to investigate treason, espionage, and sabotage

organization to gather intelligence. It also formed a Special Operations (SO) branch. Virginia Hall, who grew up in Baltimore, Maryland, joined SO in March 1944—despite having lost her lower left leg in a hunting accident years earlier. Hall helped to train three battalions of French Resistance forces to wage **guerrilla warfare** against the Nazis. Hall is famous as the only civilian woman to receive a Distinguished Service Cross during World War II for her contributions to the Allies.

The British government also had intelligence organizations during the war. Two that focused on **espionage** and sabotage were the Special Operations Executive (SOE) and the Secret Intelligence Service (SIS). Another agency, MI9, designed tools that were smuggled in to British prisoners of war (POWs) to help them escape from enemy prison camps. One MI9 employee, Christopher Clayton Hutton, was very imaginative. He designed a knife that contained a screwdriver, a lock pick, several saws, and a wire cutter. He also invented compasses hidden inside pens and shirt buttons, silk maps hidden inside canned goods, and shoes with hollow heels that could be used to stash supplies of dried food.

Nazi Germany had the Abwehr for military intelligence. Yet Hitler also turned to the Sicherheitsdienst (SD) and the Geheime Staatspolizei (Gestapo) for information, because he didn't always trust the Abwehr. The SD placed numerous agents and informants throughout German-occupied Europe to collect informa-

Dead Drops

During the war, field agents used "dead drops" to hand off and collect information. Agents used signals to indicate when information was ready to be picked up. If the drop site was a trash can, for instance, an agent might place a bottle against a nearby trash can to signal that an item was waiting.

tion on anyone suspected of being an enemy of the Nazis. The Gestapo, the Nazi secret police, spent a lot of time investigating treason, espionage, and sabotage cases. Its members quickly gained a reputation for violence. They liked to use torture to obtain information and confessions. Allied agents had to be careful of these groups.

Allied spies learned their skills at top-secret spy schools in the United States, Canada, Britain, and Scotland. One spy school was in Maryland, just 20 miles north of Washington, D.C. Another school, called Camp-X, was located in Canada, just 30 miles over the U.S. border. There, pro-Allied agents, including Canadians, Americans, Brits, Italians, Hungarians, and others, trained to acquire necessary spy skills. For example, they learned how to maintain surveillance and set up "dead drops" to hand off or collect documents and payments.

Agents also learned how to open and reseal letters, pick locks, discover if they were being followed, recruit informants, falsify documents, silently kill the enemy, and use radio transmitters. They also learned how to weave a convincing fake identity, known as a "cover," so that they

OSS gear: a blade concealed in the heel of a shoe and a dagger easily hidden.

would not cause suspicion when they got to their assignments. This meant they had to memorize many details about the life of their cover, including names of schools and employers, and the foods, drinks, customs, gestures, slang words, sports mascots, and names of trees and flowers from their cover's native country or city. Perhaps most important to their personal safety, they learned to quickly change their appearance with disguises. As a last resort, agents had the names of certain plastic surgeons who would give them a new face before they tried to sneak out of the country.

Super Spy

William Stephenson, who was born in Canada, worked as a British agent and spymaster during World War II. A spymaster is a person who directs other spies in secret missions. It was his job to help Great Britain and the United States exchange intelligence information. He also transported private information between Prime Minister Winston Churchill of Britain and President Franklin D. Roosevelt. Besides being recognized for his spying abilities, Stephenson made millions of dollars from his inventions in radio and electronics. He also won a world lightweight boxing championship, and as a fighter pilot in World War I, he shot down 26 German planes.

Make Your Own
Secret Boiled Egg Message

Some agents during the war hid secret messages in boiled eggs! In this project you'll do this using two items that are available in your grocery store's spice aisle: alum and vinegar. As you write on the egg shell with this mixture, you leave behind messages that can only be seen once you remove the shell! How is this possible? Well, the vinegar dissolves the calcium carbonate in the eggshell, allowing the alum to pass through the shell and discolor the egg white.

1 With an adult's help, hard boil a dozen eggs. Place the eggs in the water and bring water to a boil. Set your timer so that the eggs simmer for 12 minutes. Here's a tip: Add some salt to the water, as it helps make the eggs peel easier.

2 Have your mom or dad drain the hot water and rinse the eggs in cold water. Place them in a bowl or back in their carton, and put them in the refrigerator to cool.

3 In a small bowl, mix the white vinegar and alum together to form a paste.

4 Hold an egg in one hand by your thumb and forefinger while you write a message. Use the Q-tip like a pencil, dipping it into the paste.

5 Store the egg in the refrigerator overnight so the message will have time to seep through the shell and set. Peel the shell off the egg to read your secret message! You'll notice that some eggs are finicky, so this trick doesn't always work. Try a few and some will be successful!

supplies

- ✪ **12 hardboiled eggs**
- ✪ **¼ teaspoon salt**
- ✪ **2 tablespoons white vinegar**
- ✪ **2 tablespoons alum**
- ✪ **Q-tips**

Make Your Own
Footprint Mold

In this activity you'll make rubbery molds of your own feet, then fill the molds with plaster to make hard casts. This project is cool—you'll finally see what the bottom of your feet look like!

1 Place your feet in the disposable foil pans. Bend the pans around your feet so that there is only an inch or so between your foot and the side of the pan. This gives you a deep, rather than wide, "well" for your foot.

2 Assemble your items around you. First you'll mix the molds, then set your feet in them until it becomes rubbery, and then fill your feet impressions with plaster.

3 Cover your working area with newspaper. Measure the molding compound and water according to the directions on the can. Mix well with a whisk, adding the powder a little at a time. Be sure to remove any lumps.

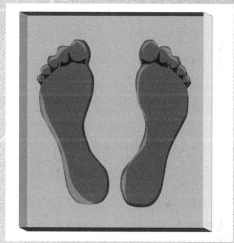

supplies

○ **2 disposable foil pans that are just a little bigger than each of your feet (available in your grocery store)**

○ **newspaper**

○ **face mask or bandana so you don't breathe in any plaster dust**

○ **measuring cups, bowl, and whisk**

○ **can of Activa Instamold molding compound OR Webster 3-D Gel (found in craft stores)**

○ **Webster microwaveable plaster of paris OR Webster strong cast plaster (super strong plaster)**

SAFETY WARNING:

NEVER put your foot directly into a mold of plaster of paris. Why? Because plaster heats up as it sets. If your foot is in the plaster, you'll get burned. That's why you need to make the mold from the molding compound, which is completely safe for you to use.

4 Put the foil pans on the floor in front of a chair. Pour the molding compound equally into both pans. It will be runny at this point.

5 Sit in your chair and place your bare feet into the molding compound. You'll need to sit because you don't want your feet to sink to the bottom of the mold. You might have to put your hands under your knees to help support the weight of your legs. Wait for 5 to 10 minutes for the mold to set. You'll know it is set when it turns rubbery. Gently remove your feet. They'll come away easily.

6 Mix the plaster. Make sure to put on your face mask first. Mix as much plaster as you think you'll need, following the directions on the box. This only takes a minute.

7 Carefully spoon or pour the plaster into the rubbery molds. Tap to remove air bubbles.

8 Wait an hour, then carefully lift your plaster impressions from their rubbery molds. Turn them over to see the soles. Note: you can reuse the molds up to six times, but they need to be stored properly. Follow the storage directions on the can.

9 Let the feet dry at least 24 hours, so they're rock hard before you use them.

10 To make tracks, "walk" them through sand or loose dirt by holding them in your hands. You can't actually walk on the plaster, because it will break.

WWII INVENTIONS

Walkie-Talkie

Just before the war U.S. inventor Al Gross invented and patented a mobile, hand-held radio that operated on frequencies above 100 megahertz (MHz). He called his two-way radio the "walkie-talkie." These lightweight, battery-operated radios were used mostly by foot soldiers to communicate with their units over short distances of no more than a mile.

PRISONS OF HATE

★ **Many European Jews were killed during World War II simply because they** were Jewish. At first the U.S. government did not allow many Jewish refugees to enter the United States, in part because of strong anti-Semitic (anti-Jewish) feelings among some in the government. Finally, in 1943, President Roosevelt established a government agency called the War Refugee Board (WRB) to help rescue Jewish refugees. The WRB help to save about 200,000 Jews.

The Nazis imprisoned Jews and others it considered "enemies of the state" in concentration camps scattered throughout Germany and Poland. These camps were known for their harsh conditions, where survival was very difficult. Families were separated from each other, many never to see each other again. One of the worst places a European Jew could end up was in an extermination camp like Auschwitz, an isolated Nazi camp in Poland. Located on the Krakow-Vienna rail

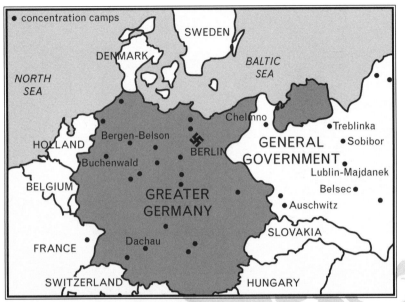

Anne Frank

line, Auschwitz was perfectly situated to receive large train shipments of prisoners. The Nazis prepared the camps by renovating the old army barracks, adding barbed wire, electrified fences, sentry towers, and vicious dogs. The Nazis put German convicts in the camps as guards.

Thousands of Jews were killed with poison gas at Auschwitz, beginning in 1942. Women, children, and old people were often immediately killed in gas chambers after their arrival at Auschwitz. It is believed that about 1.5 million people—including non-Jewish Poles, gypsies, and homosexuals—were killed by the Nazis before Allied forces liberated Auschwitz in 1945.

Anne Frank is perhaps the most recognized victim of the Nazi concentration camps because of the diary she left behind. She lived with her family in Amsterdam, the Netherlands. Anne started writing her diary at age 13, on the day she heard the Dutch minister say that after the war all diaries and letters about the war would be collected.

Unwelcome Passengers

On June 6, 1939, the German passenger ship *St. Louis* was turned away by U.S. officials. The boat, loaded with more than 900 Jewish refugees holding Cuban landing permits, was forced to return to Europe after Cuba, and then the United States, refused to let it dock. Imagine how you would feel if you were on that boat, knowing you'd be returning to the violence and fear you'd so desperately tried to escape. Belgium, the Netherlands, Great Britain, and France agreed to take the refugees, but hundreds of these passengers eventually died in Nazi concentration camps.

Anne and her family, along with four other people, spent 25 months during World War II living secretly in rooms above her father's office, in order to avoid the concentration camps. Unfortunately, the Nazis learned of their hiding place when it was discovered by some nosy workmen. In March 1945, just 9 months after she was arrested, Anne died of typhus and starvation at Bergen-Belsen, a concentration camp located in northern Germany. She was just 15. In her family, only her father survived. Found by a family friend, her diary was published in 1947. Since then her diary has been translated into 67 languages! Although Anne did not live to see it, she achieved her goal of becoming a published journalist and famous writer.

★ WWII trivia ★

On October 18, 1945, in Nuremberg, Germany, 22 of Nazi Germany's leaders were charged with war crimes and crimes against humanity. Twelve were eventually sentenced to death in the **Nuremberg Trials.**

Danish Jews

There are many amazing stories of people putting themselves at risk during World War II to save the lives of others. On September 28, 1943, a German diplomat told a Danish official about Nazi plans to round up the Danish Jews and deport them to concentration camps. Within hours, the Danish government organized a nationwide effort to inform, hide, and then smuggle the Jewish population of roughly 8,000 people to Sweden.

The following day, most of Denmark's Jews were warned of the looming danger and urged to go into hiding during religious services for Rosh Hashanah, an important Jewish holiday. Danish officials teamed up with civilians and friends to call anyone and everyone in the phonebook with a Jewish name.

Alerted of the approaching danger, Danish Jews fled their homes and sought out hiding places in other people's homes, in hospitals, and in churches. Most of them hid for several days before traveling across the Sound, a 10-mile stretch of water that separates Denmark from Sweden. All but about 800 of Denmark's Jews were ferried to safety by Danish fishermen within two weeks. Another 300 Jews attempted the trek by rowboat or kayak.

The courageous effort by the Danish saved most of Denmark's Jewish population. Unfortunately a few people were picked up by the Nazis in the middle of the Sound, and 450 others were caught before they had the chance to flee. Thanks to Danish political pressure, however, those who were caught were deported to the Terezin ghetto in Czechoslovakia, which was not a death camp.

Make Your Own
Wish Wheel Mobile

In this project you will use origami, an art form that uses folded paper, to make a wish-wheel mobile. What makes this mobile special is that each wish wheel offers you space to write a message. Some people believe that wishes will be answered if the words flutter in the wind.

1 With the printed side of the paper facing down, fold the origami paper in half in both directions, and then diagonally in both directions, opening it after each fold. With the first two folds you create rectangles. With the second two folds, you create triangles.

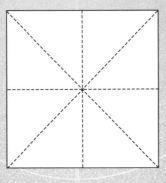

2 With the paper unfolded and flat, printed side down, fold the left side of the paper in to meet the middle fold. Unfold. Now do the same with the right side and unfold.

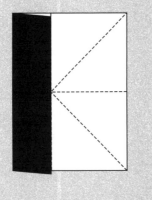

3 Flip the paper over so that the printed side is facing up. Fold each corner in to meet at the center. On each triangle, write a wish or short message. Unfold so that the paper is flat.

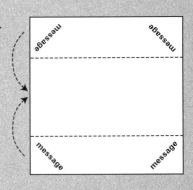

4 Turn the paper over again, so the printed side is down. Fold the top and bottom quarters of the paper in so they

supplies

- ✪ 3 pieces of origami paper or scrap wrapping paper that are 5⅞ inches square
- ✪ ⅛-inch-diameter wooden dowel
- ✪ regular or metallic thread (metallic thread will give your mobile more sparkle)
- ✪ scissors
- ✪ sewing needle with large enough eye that you can easily thread it
- ✪ suction cup for hanging mobile in window **OR** hook

meet on the middle line. Your paper looks like a rectangle.

5 Push the middle of the side in to the center, letting the corners open out. Your paper now looks like an arrow pointing to the right, although the point is missing. Do this to the left side of the paper as well. Your paper now looks like a square with triangles attached to the top and bottom.

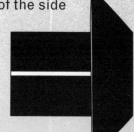

6 Grasp the right top section and fold down. Grasp the bottom left section and fold up. You now have your wish wheel, which is a pinwheel shape. Make two more pinwheels, so that you have a total of three.

7 Thread your needle, then use it to poke a hole through the square section of the wish wheel. Pull the thread through the hole.

8 Tie the thread to the dowel. Repeat with the other two wish wheels. Vary the thread so that the wheels hang at different lengths. You can slip a dab of glue under the thread, where it meets the dowel, to keep it from moving. Tie another piece of thread at the center of the dowel to hang your mobile.

9 Hang from your window or in a doorway. As your wish wheels flutter, watch to see if your wish is carried away by the wind.

CODE BREAKERS
& TALKERS

★ **The danger in sending and receiving military messages in a time of war** is the possibility that the message will fall into enemy hands. Recognizing this, the Axis powers relied on complex "ciphers" throughout World War II to keep their military messages top secret. A **cipher** is a form of code that adds or substitutes letters or numbers in a message to disguise it. In its coded form, the message appears to be gibberish—unless the person receiving the message has the proper equipment and a code book to unscramble and read it.

Early in the war Japan and Germany were successful at keeping their codes secret, which led them to believe that their complex cipher machines were unbeatable. They were wrong. The United States and Britain managed to crack their codes. Not only that—the Allies used the cipher machines to send false information back to the Axis to mislead them. This kind of deception is a form of **counterespionage**.

Japan's cipher system, the Purple Code, was invented sometime in the 1930s. The Japanese government began using it in 1939. Basically, the system included two typewriters that were wired to a cipher box. A character typed on the first typewriter sent an electrical signal to the cipher box, which then selected

Germany's cipher machine, Enigma.

Know Your WWII Words

cipher: a method of putting text in code to hide its meaning, like writing 1 for A, 2 for B, etc., or F for A, S for B

counterespionage: the discovery and defeat of enemy espionage

encode: to transfer information from one system of communication into another

decode: to convert a message in code back into ordinary language

a different character that was typed out on the second typewriter.

Germany's cipher machine was called Enigma. It was developed in 1923 to **encode** business secrets, but the German government adapted Enigma to send messages between Hitler and his military. Like the Purple Code, the Enigma used a typewriter-like contraption—based on a complicated set of rotor wheels that produced a code of not thousands, but trillions of variations—to encode and **decode** messages. The coded messages were so scrambled that only a recipient with an Enigma machine fixed to the same settings could decode it.

So how, then, did the Allied intelligence communities manage to crack these complex codes? By assigning a lot of smart people to the task. They recognized clues that sloppy Japanese and German operators put in their transmissions. And they managed to obtain copies of the cipher machines themselves.

The Signals Intelligence Service (SIS), the U.S. Army's super-secret code-breaking division in Virginia, cracked the Purple Code early in the war, in 1940. Two of the country's top code breakers, William Friedman and Frank B. Rowlett, were put in charge of this secret decoding operation, which had a code name of its own: Magic. It took Friedman, Rowlett, and their support team 18 months to crack the cipher system after they built a replica of the Japanese cipher

Kasiski Frequency Chart

A cryptogram is text written in code to keep it secret. Until the nineteenth century, simple cryptograms were used quite effectively. But they became easy to break in 1863 when a Prussian military officer by the name of Kasiski developed a table called a frequency chart. This chart identified how often a certain letter appeared in a given number of words. In the English language, for example, the letter E is used more than any other letter. In fact, for every 1,000 words, the letter E is used 591 times, but the letter Z is used only three times. Kasiski's chart made it obvious to the world that complex codes were needed, which sent the world's militaries scrambling to design codes that couldn't be easily broken.

Navajo Code Talkers Win Congressional Gold Medal

The U.S. government did not tell the American public about the Navajo code talkers. It even asked the code talkers to keep their role in the war a secret, in case they were needed in the future—and some were later used during the Vietnam War. So these men were not publicly recognized or thanked by the U.S. military until 1969. In 1971, President Richard Nixon awarded the code talkers a special certificate, and in 1982, the U.S. Senate passed a motion declaring August 14, 1982, National Code Talkers Day. On July 26, 2001, Congress bestowed one of its highest honors, the Congressional Gold Medal, on the 29 original Navajo code talkers who developed the unbreakable military code that helped the United States to win World War II. The Congressional Silver Medal was awarded to more than 300 who enlisted later in the war.

machine. Soon, the U.S. military was able to monitor Japan's coded messages. In 1942, the United States used the cipher machine to help defeat the Japanese Navy at the crucial Battle of Midway, in the Pacific.

Britain's top mathematicians, scientists, and linguists, aided by American code breakers, focused on cracking Enigma. In all, more than 7,000 men and women participated in Operation Ultra. They worked at the super-secret Government Code and Cipher School, 40 miles outside London. The code breakers got lucky when the British government was able to obtain a number of Enigma machines and copies of code books from German submarines, called U-boats. By 1945, almost all Enigma messages could be read within a day or two, giving the Allies an advantage. The Allies carefully kept Operation Ultra a secret so the Germans wouldn't know that their code had been broken.

Understanding Axis secret messages helped the Allies to win the war.

Yet the United States had trouble keeping its own message transmissions secret—until it began using Navajo and Comanche "code talkers." The code talkers were recruited from American Indian reservations. They created new radio codes based on their descriptive native languages. Birds, for example, became code names for various types of planes. The sparrow hawk (gini in Navajo), which dives when hunting for food, represented dive-bomber planes. Bombs were called a-ye-shi, which means "eggs." Navajo code talkers were effective because few people outside the Navajo tribe spoke the language fluently—and

★ WWII trivia ★

Comanche code talkers referred to Adolf Hitler as Po-sah-tie-vaw, which means "crazy white man."

Navajo Code Talkers' Dictionary

ENGLISH	NAVAJO WORD	LITERAL TRANSLATION
REGIMENT	TABAHA	EDGE WATER
PLATOON	HAS-CLISH-NIH	MUD
SQUAD	DEBEH-LI-ZINI	BLACK SHEEP
DIVE BOMBER	GINI	CHICKEN HAWK
FIGHTER PLANE	DA-HE-TIH-HI	HUMMINGBIRD
BOMBER PLANE	JAY-SHO	BUZZARD
BATTLESHIP	LO-TSO	WHALE
AIRCRAFT	TSIDI-MOFFA-YE-HI	BIRD CARRIER
SUBMARINE	BESH-LO	IRON FISH
GRENADE	NI-MA-SI	POTATOES
SABOTEUR	A-TKEL-EL-INI	TROUBLE MAKER

there is no written form of the language. It is almost impossible for an adult to learn and master the Navajo language. Every syllable has a meaning, and differences in tone of voice change the meaning of individual sentences.

The Navajo code talkers began operating in the Pacific in 1942, totally confusing the Japanese. Similarly, when 13 Comanche code talkers landed

Navajo code talkers in the Pacific.

with Allied troops on the Normandy beaches on D-day, June 6, 1944, they confused the Germans. Why were neither of the codes broken by the Japanese or Germans during the war? Because the codes were based on oral languages so complex that few people outside the Comanche and Navajo tribes knew them.

Make Your Own
Code Grill

One of the easiest ways to hide a secret message is by using a code grill. To write the message, you simply hide words within other words. The message is easily read by a person who places the grill on top of the message. The holes in the grill highlight the secret words, while blocking out the rest of the text.

1 On a scrap piece of paper, write out your message so you won't forget it.

2 On one of the pieces of paper, carefully rewrite your message. You are doing this for placement only. Be sure to space the words randomly, using the full sheet of paper, leaving plenty of room around each word.

3 Draw rectangles around your words, then cut them out. If you hold the paper up, your words are gone, but that's what you want. This piece of paper is your code grill.

4 Lay your code grill on top of the second piece of paper. In the holes, carefully rewrite your message. Be sure not to use any capital letters in your message, because they will make the words in your message more noticeable.

5 Remove the code grill. You should easily be able to read your message on the underlying piece of paper. Now you need to hide it! Fill in words or letters around your secret message, until you have filled the page. It should now look like a page of gibberish, or sentences that don't make sense.

6 Now lay your code grill over the message page. Voila! The gibberish is covered by the page, while only your secret message appears in the holes you cut out!

7 Give copies of your code grill to your friends. You can use it to write secret messages to each other and then decode them. If your messages fall into enemy hands your secrets will be safe.

topdstesecretemsmeeting
atponoonstemacrosstops
theonestreetatfromonthe
publicweblibrarybookand
waitstepformlarvadosignal

supplies

- ✪ scrap piece of paper
- ✪ pen or pencil
- ✪ 2 pieces of paper
- ✪ scissors

Make Your Own

Signal Light to Send Coded Messages

If you're not close enough to a friend to actually hear what he or she is saying, and you can't find a phone or a way to send a letter, how might you communicate? By flicking a light switch, of course! In this project you'll make your own portable signal device using the power from a battery. Add Morse code, and you'll be sending—and receiving—messages in no time.

1 Divide your supplies into two, as you have enough to make two signal lights.

2 Tape a piece of copper wire to each end of the two batteries using the black electrical tape.

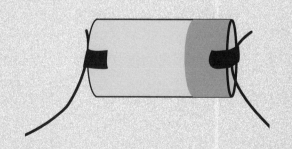

3 Screw each bulb into the bulb holder. Use a screwdriver to attach the free ends of the copper wires to the two screws on the base of each bulb holder. Your bulbs should light up.

4 Select one of the copper wires and use the pliers or wire cutters to cut the wire about 3 inches from where the wire is attached to the bulb holder.

5 You now have two free ends, which will attach to your switch. Loop the shorter end around one of the thumbtacks and press the tack into the wood block.

supplies

- ✪ 2 "C" batteries
- ✪ 4 pieces of bare copper wire, each about 10 inches long
- ✪ 6 inches of black electrical tape, cut into four strips
- ✪ 2 small bulbs with threaded base
- ✪ 2 bulb holders
- ✪ screwdriver
- ✪ pliers or wire cutters
- ✪ 4 thumbtacks
- ✪ 2 small metal paper clips
- ✪ 2 square blocks of scrap wood, about 4 inches wide by 4 inches long
- ✪ 2 Morse code alphabet cheat sheets

6 Loop the remaining free end of copper wire around the other tack. Before you press it into the wood, hook it through one end of the metal paper clip, so that the end of the clip is underneath the head of the tack. The tacks should be placed just far enough apart for the paper clip to swing between the thumbtacks, touching both tacks when in the "closed" position.

7 Repeat steps 4, 5, and 6 for the other signal light. How does the signal switch work? When you "close" the system, by having the paper clip touch both thumbtacks, the bulb will light up. When you swing the paper clip away from the second thumbtack, the system is "open" and battery current can not reach the bulb, so the light goes out.

8 With a friend, use Morse code to send messages back and forth. Turn the light on briefly for a dot, longer for a dash. Practice first with the international distress signal: SOS. You can also make up a shorthand code of your own so that you don't have to spell out individual letters.

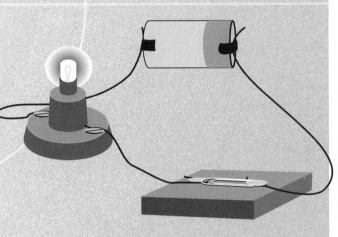

Morse Code Alphabet

A	.-	L	.-..	W	.--	6	-....
B	--...	M	--	X	-..-	7	--...
C	-.-.	N	-.	Y	-.--	8	---..
D	-..	O	---	Z	--..	9	----.
E	.	P	.--.				
F	..-.	Q	--.-	**Numbers**		**Full Stop**	
G	--.	R	.-.	0	-----	.-.-.-	
H	....	S	...	1	.----		
I	..	T	-	2	..---	**Comma**	
J	.---	U	..-	3	...--	--..--	
K	-.-	V	...-	4	....-		
				5	.....	**Query**	..

LIFTING
MORALE

The American soldiers who fought on the front lines during World War II had lots to worry about—not just the constant reminder that, at any moment, they could be injured or killed. They also worried about their families and about the businesses and jobs they had left behind. Some soldiers worried that their sweethearts had forgotten them. Others wondered about their new babies— they might not even have met them. Hands down, American GIs wanted just one thing: for the Allies to quickly win the war. That done, they could get back to their homes, families, and jobs.

Recognizing the importance of lifting troop **morale**, the military gave its fighters plenty of food, good medical care, and opportunities for entertainment—such as movies, radio broadcasts, card games, baseball games, and USO shows. When possible, they even sent the GIs home on temporary leaves. And the government made sure the soldiers, sailors, and pilots received the many letters written by their loved ones back home. Because paper was rationed, however, and large bundles of letters were expensive to ship to Europe and

Navy pilots aboard USS Monterey in the forward elevator well playing basketball.

the Pacific, the government asked (but did not require) American civilians to use a letter format called "V-mail" or victory mail.

Civilians bought special V-mail forms at their local drugstores and post offices. They filled out the limited space on the form, much like we would write on a postcard. After the government received the forms and cleared the content through a **censor**, V-mail was photographed and the film was sent overseas by plane. Film was much lighter than paper and took up a lot less space. But just how much space and weight? According to the National Postal Museum, the 37 mailbags required to carry 150,000 one-page letters were replaced by a single V-mail sack. And the weight dropped from 2,575 pounds to just 45 pounds. Now that makes a difference!

Once V-mail arrived in Europe or the Pacific, the film was printed out and each letter was sent to the GI it was addressed to. The whole process typically took about two weeks.

Although V-mail arrived much quicker than regular mail, which often took six weeks to reach the Pacific or Europe

Allotment Annie

Some young American women participated in a wartime swindle, by marrying more than one man. These girls were referred to as "Allotment Annies" because they married two, three, or more soldiers, sailors, or pilots in order to receive part of their husband's monthly military pay or allotment from the U.S. Treasury Department. Why risk getting caught? These women were greedy, hoping to collect on a husband's $10,000 life insurance policy if he was killed in battle.

Know Your WWII Words

morale: sense of purpose and usefulness, confidence in the future

censor: someone who checked the mail to make sure nothing in it would harm the country or the war effort

by boat, many American civilians continued to send regular paper letters to their loved ones. Families also sent care packages. These boxes of cookies, cakes, hand-knit scarves, cigarettes, matches, razor blades, and toothbrushes brought smiles to the troops and reminded them that they were supported and missed. Between June 15, 1942, and April 1, 1945, more than 550 million pieces of V-mail were sent from U.S. civilians to military post offices. More than 510 million pieces of return mail were sent from the troops fighting in Europe and the Pacific.

The military also allowed units to have pet dogs as their mascots, knowing the animals cheered up the men and gave them something to care about. Some dogs were found and adopted by GIs after they got to Europe and the Pacific. Soldiers even made pets of goats, cats, pigs, and snakes! The military also formally trained dogs, mostly Labradors, German shepherds, and Doberman pinschers, to support the troops as trackers, scouts, and messengers, and to use their excellent sense of smell to sniff out booby traps and mines. The War Dog Program was formally started in 1942. Many of the dogs were donated by American families.

Yummy C Rations!

Even when there was no place to set up a kitchen, the U.S. military made sure that American GIs in World War II had enough food. Soldiers soon grew to appreciate the military's pre-made food kits, called C rations (Meal, Combat Individual). Today they're called MREs (Meal, Ready to Eat, Individual). The C Rations certainly weren't as tasty or satisfying as a fresh, hot meal. But they provided enough nutrition to keep the soldiers in good fighting condition. Even if the soldiers didn't particularly care for the main course, they knew they'd always find something sweet, such as M&Ms, gum, or jelly, and a packet of instant coffee.

WWII INVENTIONS

M&M Candies

Forrest Edward Mars of the Mars candy company developed M&Ms, which were distributed to soldiers by the U.S. Army. The "melt in your mouth, not in your hand" candies were perfect for soldiers because the candy's hard coating kept the chocolate from melting and making the soldiers' hands sticky.

⭐ **WWII trivia** ⭐

After World War II, surviving war dogs were sent home to their families with honorable discharges.

By 1945, nearly 10,000 dogs had been trained and distributed to units in both Europe and the Pacific. These brave dogs saved the lives of many Allied soldiers.

While the U.S. military spent a lot of effort keeping troop morale high, the Axis powers tried really hard to keep it low. One way they did so was through "black" propaganda. Black propaganda messages seemed to offer concern and support, but their real aim was to embarrass the soldiers and make them feel bad through half-truths and lies. Some of these messages were on leaflets and postcards dropped by enemy pilots. The leaflets expressed sorrow over high Allied casualty rates and encouraged the GIs to enjoy their "short lives." They also said that Allied soldiers shouldn't worry too much about their sweethearts back home, because they were happily dating other men. Japan and Germany aired daily propaganda radio programs that contained enough inside knowledge of Allied strategy to make the Allies take notice—and American civilians listening back home worry.

Mildred Gillars, called "Axis Sally," broadcast German radio propaganda programs from a Berlin radio station.

News correspondents interview captured "Tokyo Rose" in September 1945.

Would it surprise you to learn that two of these radio programs were hosted by American-born women? Mildred Gillars, nicknamed Axis Sally, made the broadcasts for Radio Berlin in Nazi Germany. Iva Toguri, whom the Allies called Tokyo Rose, broadcast from Tokyo. Fortunately for the Allies, neither woman had much negative influence on the Allied troops. In fact, the troops thought they were funny because they said such ridiculous things!

In 1935 Gillars had moved to Germany, where she became an English instructor at the Berlitz School of Languages in Berlin. Her propaganda program, known as "Home

Goals or Strategies of Propagandists

✪ Instill fear in a group of people to build mass support. For example, the Nazis warned the German people that the Allies wanted to wipe them out.

✪ Repeat the same claim over and over, until it is finally accepted as truth.

✪ Account for actions, even bad ones, by using vague and pleasant-sounding phrases.

✪ Use influential, respected people like movie stars to make statements that will persuade others to act in a certain way.

✪ Find scapegoats and blame problems on them. The Nazis blamed the Jews for Germany's problems, which convinced the public to view them negatively.

✪ Use catchy slogans. The U.S. Government, for example, popularized the phrase "Loose Lips Sink Ships" to remind Americans not to engage in idle chatter, particularly with strangers.

Wooden receiving aerial towers with transmitter towers to the rear.

Sweet Home" aired each day, from December 11, 1941, through May 6, 1945. She referred to herself as "Midge at the Mike," but American GIs called her "Axis Sally." Toguri, who identified herself as "Orphan Ann" on the radio, got stuck in Tokyo just after the attack on Pearl Harbor when she was visiting family. After the war, Toguri admitted that she made the propaganda broadcasts, but argued that she was forced to do so by the Japanese because she spoke English. The U.S. government decided that both women were guilty of treason and put them in prison.

WWII INVENTIONS

Ribbon Microphone

This microphone was invented in 1942 for radio broadcasting. Microphones convert sound waves into electrical voltages that are converted back into sound waves through speakers. Hitler effectively used microphones during his large public radio addresses, amplifying his voice so thousands could hear his messages of promise and hate.

Make Your Own
Ration Kit

1 Ration kits are made up of canned or pre-packaged foods and drinks. Make a list of your favorites. For each item, list the calories, grams of fat, grams of protein, grams of carbohydrates, and milligrams of sodium. If the foods are not in your kitchen pantry, go to the grocery store to get this information. Your goal is to put together a kit for two days with about 1,800 calories a day, and with fewer than 2,000 milligrams of sodium a day, so you won't get too thirsty.

2 Using your chart, decide which foods you will eat for breakfast, lunch, dinner, and snacks. Each meal needs to be healthy, and include roughly equal amounts of protein and carbohydrates. Remember to count the calories from any fruit drinks.

3 Bag each meal separately in a plastic bag. Write the day and meal on each bag. Place the items in your box or backpack. Make sure to include enough water. You need to drink at least eight, 8-ounce glasses of water a day.

4 Enjoy your two days of rations! Can you think of ways to make your ration kits more nutritious? How about more enjoyable? Don't just add more candy—remember a soldier needs good nutrition to stay fit and healthy.

supplies

- ✪ cardboard box **OR** backpack
- ✪ prepackaged food that does not need refrigeration such as granola bars, beef jerky, candy bars, cheese and peanut butter crackers, pretzels, dried fruit, nuts, Vienna sausages, instant soup, peanut butter, canned tuna, canned fruit, etc.
- ✪ water and other drinks

Make Your Own
Soldier Care Package

In this project, you'll make a care package for a soldier currently stationed outside of the United States. Carry on, civilian, your country needs you!

1 First, order your free U.S. Postal Service–approved shipping boxes to make sure your package isn't rejected by the post office. You need the "Care Kit 04." You must be at least 18 years old to order the kit, so ask an adult to place the call. The number is 1-800-610-8734. Press "1" for express mailing. A postal clerk will record your mom or dad's name, phone number, and address, and put the kit in the mail.

2 When the kit arrives at your house, decide which boxes or envelopes you want to use. Even the tape, mailing labels, and customs forms you need are included!

supplies

- ✪ **Care Kit 04**
- ✪ **prepackaged food items such as cookies, candy bars, gum, fruit cups, raisins, Doritos, Slim Jims, salted peanuts, sunflower seeds, Tang, Gatorade, Starburst candy, Skittles, and Kool-Aid (but no pork or pork products if you are sending the package to a Muslim country, which forbids the consumption of pork)**
- ✪ **prepackaged hygiene items such as disposable razors, deodorant, a comb, lip balm with SPF 15, Kleenex, and Q-Tips, or maybe even a pair of socks**
- ✪ **some type of activity book, such as a crossword puzzle book or joke book**
- ✪ **something to make the soldier laugh, such as a silly story or funny picture**
- ✪ **a letter introducing yourself and saying why you're sending the package**

3 The military requires that packages be addressed to individual soldiers. But you get to pick the soldier! One way is to go on the Internet to www.anysoldier.com. Click the "Where to send" button. Scroll through the list of names. Each soldier listed offers ideas for the items he or she would most like to receive.

4 Decide if you are sending a "food" package or a "hygiene" package. Don't mix these items, as the chemical smell of things like soap and deodorant will make the food items taste terrible. You can add books, photographs, and your letter to either box. Seal the box and wrap it in A LOT of tape. It will be handled by a lot of people before it gets to the solider.

5 Fill out the mailing label very carefully, using the address provided by the soldier you picked. Ask your parents for help or to check it when you finish. You must copy the address exactly.

6 You must also fill out a customs form so the post office knows what is inside your care package. Ask your parents for help if you need it. The post office will not accept your package without a customs form.

7 Go to the post office to send your package. You might have to use some of your allowance for shipping! Your package should reach your soldier in a couple of weeks.

8 Don't expect a reply, as soldiers are busy fighting the war. But you can bet the soldier who gets your letter has read it. Congratulations! You've just helped to raise soldier morale!

Care package drive at Hanscom's Air Force Base.

PROVING THEIR
VALUE

During World War II, American society was still segregated. Segregated means separated, and black people and white people lived very separate lives in the 1940s. In many parts of the country there were "Whites Only" signs on bathrooms, water fountains, restaurants, libraries, and even movie theaters. Laws that legalized this **segregation**, called Jim Crow Laws, allowed this to happen. African Americans faced **discrimination** and **prejudice** on a daily basis. They had to live with the same discrimination in the military.

Initially, African American servicemen were only allowed to have certain jobs, such as in kitchens and motor pools. An airplane cockpit was off limits! But there was pressure on the government to expand the role of African Americans in the military. Public Law 18 passed on April 3, 1939. It specifically called for training programs at black colleges to prepare African Americans for military service. The Army Air Corps took up the challenge. The country's first African American military pilots, known as the "Tuskegee Airmen" would soon prove their ability and **valor** to both the U.S. military and civilians.

Tuskegee Airmen in flight gear.

On January 9, 1941, Secretary of War Henry L. Stimson approved an all-black flight training program at Tuskegee Institute, a small college in Tuskegee, Alabama. Charles Alfred Anderson, the nation's first African American to earn a commercial transport pilot's license, directed the program. The 99th Fighter Squadron was formed to see if black pilots could successfully fly in combat. Today it seems incredible that this would be a question, but that shows how society has changed.

Interested young African American men from all over the country applied for the program, eager to prove their ability. By 1946 more than 2,000 men had completed the training. More than half of them qualified as pilots. In Europe, the squadron excelled in protecting bomber planes. It quickly became famous for its impressive combat record against the German fighter planes. The 99th earned the respect of the Luftwaffe, who began calling these men the "Schwarze Vogelmenschen" or Black Birdmen.

On July 4, 1944, the 99th combined with three other all-black squadrons that had trained at Tuskegee—the 100th, the 301st, and the 302nd—to form the 332nd Fighter Group. The 332nd switched to their signature aircraft, the P-51 Mustang, and used bright red paint to decorate their plane tails. They quickly earned the nickname "Redtails." These pilots were the only

Take Me Up!

In 1941, First Lady Eleanor Roosevelt visited Tuskegee Army Air Field to learn how well African Americans flew planes. When asked by flight instructor Charles A. Anderson if she wanted a test flight, she accepted—over the objections of her Secret Service agents. Anderson successfully piloted Mrs. Roosevelt over the skies of Alabama, proving to her that skin color didn't matter in the cockpit. After that, Mrs. Roosevelt threw her full support behind the "Tuskegee Experiment."

P-51 Mustang.

WWII trivia ✪

Airmen on Film

✪ In 1995 HBO memorialized the Airmen in a made-for-TV movie titled *The Tuskegee Airmen*. Starring Laurence Fishburne, it is rated PG-13.

✪ In 2008, Hollywood plans to release a film about the Airmen titled *Red Tails*.

✪ PBS created a 1-hour documentary titled *The Tuskegee Airmen*.

Notable Bravery

Here are just two examples of the bravery shown by African American servicemen during World War II:

During the attack on Pearl Harbor, U.S. Navy Mess Attendant Doris (Dorie) Miller helped to move his mortally wounded commander to shelter, then manned a machine gun on the USS *West Virginia*, shooting at Japanese aircraft. He is widely credited with shooting down a plane—an incredible achievement. Miller did so without any formal training on the machine gun, because combat positions were not open to black sailors. The navy eventually awarded Miller the Navy Cross during a ceremony on May 27, 1942. Unfortunately, Miller was killed in 1943 when the Japanese torpedoed the USS *Liscombe Bay*. In 1973, the navy commissioned the destroyer escort USS *Miller* in recognition of Miller's bravery.

Later in the war, Private Warren Capers was part of the 320th Negro Anti-Aircraft Barrage Balloon Battalion, the only African-American combat troops to take part in the D-day landings on the beaches of Normandy, France, on June 6, 1944. Capers helped to set up a dressing station that treated more than 330 soldiers. He was awarded a Silver Star.

fighter group that did not lose a bomber to Axis fighters during the war. They also destroyed more than 260 German airplanes, and 950 railcars and motor vehicles. Their greatest contribution, though, was proving that their skin color was not a factor in their capability. Their bravery and accomplishments led to desegregation in the military.

About 450 of the African American pilots trained in Tuskegee **deployed** overseas. They made thousands of sorties, which are short missions. Thirty-two were held as POWs and 66 lost their lives in combat.

After the war, in 1948, President Harry S. Truman signed Executive Order 9981, which guaranteed equality of treatment and opportunity despite the color of a person's skin. Segregation officially ceased in the military, although discrimination continued to linger for many years. Truman's action was guided, in large part, by the bravery and skill shown by African American servicemen during World War II.

442nd Infantry Regimental Combat Team.

Japanese Americans also proved their loyalty to the United States, when the government finally allowed them to enlist in the military. Army recruiters visited the Japanese internment camps in 1943, offering military service to the young men imprisoned there as a way to show their loyalty. Japanese Americans were not allowed to serve in combat roles against Japan in the fight in the Pacific. But some did serve in Asia as spies, translators, interpreters, and POW interrogators. Like German Americans and Italian Americans who were sent to the Pacific, their work helped America win many important battles against Japan. It saved the lives of American soldiers, and ended the war more quickly.

The U.S. Army asked Japanese Americans living in Hawaii for 1,500 volunteers, and about 10,000 signed up. About 1,200 Japanese Americans living in mainland internment camps signed up. These men formed the 442nd Infantry Regimental Combat Team, which fought bravely in Europe against the Axis enemies. This unit lived up to its motto of "Go For Broke," risking everything to gain the respect of America. It became one of the most highly decorated units in the history of the U.S. Army, earning the nickname "Purple Heart Battalion." The men earned more than 9,000 Purple Hearts! The Purple Heart is a military decoration awarded to members of the U.S. military who have been wounded or killed in battle.

Unfortunately, their courage and bravery against Axis bullets and bombs was not enough to change the anti-Japanese views held by many Americans. When these veterans returned to America, many of them were denied service in restaurants and stores, and they had difficulty finding jobs. Some even had their homes vandalized.

Know Your WWII Words

segregation: separation of the races

discrimination: treating someone differently because of race, gender, or other characteristic

prejudice: hostility toward a race or group

valor: bravery, courage

deploy: to go to the battlefield

Make Your Own
Secret Message Deck

Spies hid maps and messages in cards to help POWs escape. Here's your chance to make your own secret messages.

1 Organize the two decks of cards into the same order by suit and number.

2 If you want to make a secret map, draw the map on a piece of paper. Fold the paper in half lengthwise, then in half again. Open your map up and smooth it out. Fold it in half widthwise, then in half again, and in half again. When you open and spread out your map it will have 32 sections.

3 Write a number from 1 to 32 on the upper left corner of each section, so the person you give it to will know in what order to arrange them. Cut the paper into 32 strips following the fold lines. The strips are small enough to be sandwiched between two cards.

4 You can fold another piece of paper in the same way and write a spy message. Since a deck of cards has 52 cards, you have room for 20 more strips.

Number these so the person you give it to can put your messages in order.

5 Glue one slip of paper onto each of the 52 cards in one deck, careful to place the paper in the center of the card. You don't need more than a dab or two of glue. Try to use as little as possible so it doesn't create a tale-tell bump.

6 Run the rubber cement brush around the edge of the card. Glue the matching card from the second deck on top of it so that the top card shows the back and the bottom card shows the front.

7 Glue all of your cards together in the same way until your deck is complete, being careful to make sure the corners are lined up perfectly so no one can tell you've "doctored" the deck!

8 Give the deck to a friend and see if he or she can put together the map and message and do what it says!

supplies

- ✪ **two decks of playing cards with the same design pattern**
- ✪ **8 ½-by-11-inch copy paper**
- ✪ **pen or marker**
- ✪ **scissors**
- ✪ **rubber cement (the kind with a brush in the bottle)**

WOMEN
IN THE DANGER ZONE

★ **World War II also gave women the opportunity to prove their intelligence,** their courage, and their muscle. Without a doubt, the war could not have been won without the help of the millions of women who worked on assembly lines and in offices. Women welded, sewed, and packed parachutes. They worked as translators, radio operators, truck drivers, typists, mechanics, lab technicians, and even postal workers. Women did the jobs left open by men sent to the battle front.

Yet, some American women wanted to contribute to the war effort by getting a whole lot closer to the action. They couldn't fight in combat units, so what were their options? Some chose to document the war as journalists, broadcasters, and photographers. Others joined the military as nurses, caring for wounded soldiers. Still others jumped into cockpits and took to the skies. More than 350,000 brave American women joined the Women's Army Corps (WAC), the Women Airforce Service Pilots (WASP), the Navy Women's Reserve, the Marine Corps Women's Reserve, the Coast Guard Women's Reserve, and the Army and Navy Nurse Corps.

Don't miss your great opportunity..

THE NAVY NEEDS YOU IN THE WAVES

Journalism in Danger

World War II journalist Helen Kirkpatrick was born in Rochester, New York, in 1909. She worked as a reporter for the *New York Tribune* and the *Chicago Daily News*, but in 1937 she moved to London. She covered the Blitz (the bombings of London by the German air force) of 1940 and accompanied the U.S. Army when it landed in Normandy, France, in 1944 in Operation Overlord.

WAC members served as radio operators, mechanics, and parachute riggers. WAVES recruits (a division of the Navy Women's Reserve) did too, but also served as control-tower operators and lots of other jobs. Some in the military worried that women would not be able to handle their jobs, but they were soon proved wrong. More than 22,000 women joined the Marine Corps, serving in more than 200 jobs, including mechanic, radio operator, mapmaker, telegraph operator, and welder. Recruiting posters aimed at women read: "Be a marine. Free a marine to fight."

The U.S. military was short of pilots. After seeing that British women were doing such a good job ferrying planes around the British Isles as part of the Air Transport Auxiliary, the

First uniform designs for Women's Army Corps.

WWII trivia

First Lady Eleanor Roosevelt fully supported American women serving as pilots during World War II. In 1942 she said, "This is not a time when women should be patient. We are in a war and we need to fight it with all our ability and every weapon possible. Women pilots, in this particular case, are a weapon waiting to be used."

United States recruited women as pilots. The WASP program was formed in 1943, though not as an official part of the military. About 1,000 women completed the rigorous training and became fully qualified pilots.

Soviet women, in comparison, were already flying military combat missions. American women were not allowed to fly combat missions but they transported planes and supplies from aircraft assembly plants and military bases to wherever the planes were needed. They also towed targets so fighter pilots could practice firing, and they trained male pilots how to fly. On December 20, 1944, when WASP was officially deactivated, its women members had flown 60 million miles in 77 types of aircraft. Thirty-three had lost their lives. Despite all that they had proven, the U.S. Air Force did not offer flying positions to women when it separated from the army in 1947. These women were not officially recognized for their efforts until 1977, when they were finally given veteran status.

After the attack on Pearl Harbor the U.S. military realized it had a huge nursing shortage. The American Red Cross immediately began recruiting unmarried women under the age of 40. By June 1942, just six months after the surprise attack at Pearl Harbor, the Army Nurse Corps had grown from less than

Life Savers

Penicillin had gained widespread use by 1943. The antibiotic was discovered by accident by British scientist Sir Alexander Fleming in 1928. The Allies also learned how to store and transport blood, which was used to give blood to the wounded. This is called a transfusion. These two innovations alone saved many lives.

Save his life... and find your own

BE A NURSE

WRITE TO STUDENT NURSES, 1790 BROADWAY, N.Y.C.

⭐ **WWII trivia** ⭐

The demand for nurses became so great during the war that the U.S. government provided free education to nursing students between 1943 and 1948.

1,000 to 12,000. About 16,000 women joined the Navy Nurse Corps. In the army alone, about 60,000 American women eventually served as nurses during the war, in both Europe and the Pacific. More than 200 of them lost their lives.

Why did American women become military nurses? Government propaganda posters showed a glamorous and exciting lifestyle. In government-sponsored films, too, nurses wore bright smiles as they drove around in jeeps and socialized. Once they joined up, nurses were shocked to discover that most of their days were hectic. Many worked in field hospitals near the front lines. Others escorted the wounded on trains, ships, and medical transport planes. They dodged bombs—and local rodents, insects, and diseases. Even though they didn't have enough supplies, these brave women tried to heal the physical and mental wounds of Allied soldiers.

Nurses sterilized bloody instruments, dispensed medications, stitched gaping wounds, and assisted with amputations. They relied on penicillin and blood transfusions to see the men through. Some of the nurses received six months of training as anesthetists. An anesthetist is someone who makes a person unconscious before an operation. It was their job to anesthetize the wounded soldiers who needed operations. The army trained other nurses to

Medical Flags

American nurses had to dodge bullets and bombs as they worked in makeshift field hospitals during World War II. Exasperated, some nurses took it upon themselves to sew large medical flags from white sheets, which they hung from windows and draped from rooftops in the hopes that the enemy would leave them—and their wounded soldiers—alone.

Broken Rules

In 1929, the world governments set up the Third Geneva Convention to make rules for the treatment of POWs. One requirement was that POW camps be open to inspection by a neutral organization or group, such as the International Red Cross. According to the convention, POWs were to be housed in heated and lighted buildings—in conditions similar to those of the captor's own troops. The convention also stated that POWs who died in the camps were to be honorably buried in marked graves. Enlisted troops were required to do whatever jobs the camp leaders gave them—as long as the jobs were not dangerous and did not support the enemy war effort. Officers were not required to work, unless they volunteered. Everyone in the camp was supposed to get at least one day of rest per week. These guidelines were often ignored by German prisons during World War II, where treatment of prisoners could be quite harsh. Treatment varied according to the nationality and race of the prisoner. British and American POWs were treated much better than Soviet POWs. In fact, most Soviet POWs died in captivity. The Soviet Union was the only major power in the war that did not sign the 1929 Geneva Convention. The Germans used this to justify their poor treatment of Soviet POWs. And the Soviets were no kinder to German prisoners. Of the 90,000 German soldiers captured at Stalingrad only 5,000 lived to return to Germany after the war. Japanese POW camps were known to be the most cruel of all, even though Japan had signed the Geneva Convention.

work with patients suffering from the mental stress of war. Some of these men couldn't handle the guilt they felt in killing others. Other soldiers became severely depressed after seeing their buddies killed in action.

American POW Camps

Throughout the war, Japan, Germany, Italy, Britain, Canada, and the United States housed prisoners of war in internment camps. At the end of World War II more than 600 POW camps were filled with more than 425,000 prisoners, located all over the United States.

For more than 60 of the army nurses, however, their greatest challenge came when they were captured by the Japanese and sent to the Santo Tomas Internment Camp in the Philippines. A handful of navy nurses were imprisoned at Los Banos Internment Camp, which the Japanese touted as a "health resort." For more than three years, these female POWs lived in desperate conditions with other camp prisoners, including civilian men, women, and children, eating watery rice and hoping for rescue. In February 1945, they were finally freed by Allied troops. General Douglas MacArthur personally shook their hands.

Make Your Own
Recruitment "Poster"

In this project, you're going to make your own recruitment poster—using cookie dough! You're sure to get a lot of attention with your edible message, which is, after all, the whole point of advertising.

1 Bake the cookie dough, following the instructions for a pan cookie. Leave it in the pan to cool.

2 When completely cool, spread some of the white icing on the cookie. But leave a 3-inch strip at the top and bottom of the cookie for colored icing. Perhaps blue icing in the top section and red icing in the bottom? Divide the remaining white icing into two bowls and add blue food coloring to one and red to the other. Mix it in well. Spread one color at the bottom and one at the top.

3 Lay horizontal strips of red licorice where the colored icings meet the white icing.

4 In the center section, on the white icing, make some stars with the sprinkles and Red Hot candies. Form the outline of the stars with the Red Hots, and fill in the centers with the sprinkles.

5 Use the tube of white icing to spell out your message. In the blue section, write NURSES NEEDED. In the red section, write JOIN UP!

6 Share your recruitment message with your friends, family, or class. But before anyone gets to eat, tell them how important nurses were during World War II.

supplies

- ✪ 1 or 2 packages of pre-made sugar- or chocolate-chip-cookie dough (in your grocery store's refrigerated section)
- ✪ large tub of white icing
- ✪ red and blue food coloring
- ✪ red licorice strings
- ✪ red and blue sprinkles
- ✪ Red Hots (cinnamon candies)
- ✪ tube of white icing (with fine tip for writing)
- ✪ any other decorations you want to add

INGENIOUS
WAR
TECHNOLOGY

★ **Throughout history, people have benefited from new technologies. Our** ancestors found life much easier after someone came up with the idea for the wheel, the loom, and the process for forging metal tools. Armies always seek out new technologies, looking for just about anything that will give them the advantage. During medieval conflicts, for example, soldiers used battering rams and trebuchets to blast through the walls of rival castles. During World War I, they used bombs and cannons.

The new technologies developed during World War II placed warfare on an entirely new level. War truly became scientific. How, for instance, was Hitler able to so easily march into Poland in 1939 and defeat the Polish army? And how did his German tanks so quickly take France, Belgium, Denmark, and the Netherlands. It's because Germans were especially good at coordinated warfare. They used their tanks with their air force planes in joint attacks. Mass production of weapons had changed the face of war long before World War II, so that fire power outweighed manpower. Germany was known for stressing high quality in its weapons production,

German Panzer tank.

which gave it an advantage. When the United States entered the war the Allies invented new weapons and factories churned them out on assembly lines. The United States was the greatest producer of weapons, a whiz at **mass production**.

C-47 transport plane.

M9A1 bazooka.

Four Allied inventions that helped win the war were the C-47 transport plane, the M9A1 shoulder-based rocket launcher (bazooka), the jeep, and the atomic bomb. Many other tools and weapons played important roles too, including the walkie-talkie, the **proximity fuse**, and the amphibious truck and tank. Even improvements to earlier technologies, such as the **barrage balloon**, radar, and sonar, contributed to success.

The United States and Britain worked together to develop new technologies. The proximity fuse was one of their joint inventions. Why was this invention important? Because proximity fuses **detonated** explosives using radio waves. This made it possible for the explosives to go off when a specific target came into range, rather than relying on an **altimeter**, a timing device, or physical contact

★ WWII trivia ★

One of the best tanks designed by Nazi Germany was the Panther, which was put into action in 1943. The Panther (Panzerkampfwagen Mark V Panther) replaced the German Panzer III and IV tanks that were too small to fight against the Soviet T-34. The Panther could travel at 28 miles per hour, and its gun was so powerful it could penetrate the armor of heavy Soviet and other Allied tanks. Between 1943 and 1945, Germany produced nearly 5,000 Panther tanks.

Pilotless "Buzz Bombs"

Pilotless flying German V-1 bombs used by the air force were particularly terrifying to their victims. These "buzz bombs" announced their presence with a shrill whistle. Fifteen seconds before they exploded, the whistle would stop. Anyone directly under the bomb when it went silent knew they were in serious trouble. The V-1 traveled at more than 400 miles per hour. When it stopped whistling it suddenly descended into a steep dive. Most of the missiles fired against London were preset to detonate over the center of the city. Germany also had V-2 rockets, which gave no warning before they detonated. From June 1944 through March 1945, Germany launched 9,251 V-1 bombs on England. Yet only 2,419 of the bombs hit their intended targets. Why? In part because 2,000 of them were shot down or knocked off course by Britain's air force, and 278 were snagged by barrage balloons!

Know Your **WWII Words**

mass production: the manufacture of products on a very large scale, usually using machines

proximity fuse: a device for firing explosives when the target comes into range

barrage balloons: balloons anchored to the ground or ships by cables that caught buzz bombs and forced attacking enemy aircraft to fly high to avoid the cables

altimeter: an instrument for measuring height

detonate: to explode or set off

sitting duck: an easy or defenseless target

U-boat: German submarine

convoy: a group organized to travel together for protection, often with military escorts

prototype: the first model of a new invention

with the target. Basically, the explosive contained a tiny radio that sent out a signal. It "listened" for its echo as it bounced off the target, increasing the chances the explosive made a damaging hit. Soon, Axis planes were **sitting ducks**!

The Allies also worked to improve radar systems, which prevented Axis planes from launching surprise attacks. The British government had patented radar before the war, based on the work of Sir Robert Alexander Watson-Watt. He got the idea to bounce a radio wave against an object to find targets. By 1939, a long chain of radar stations dotted Britain's south coast, on the watch for enemy aircraft.

The stations operated under the code name "Chain Home." They were so effective at detecting enemy aircraft at any time of day, in any kind of weather, that Britain was able to defeat Germany in the Battle of Britain in 1940. Watson-Watt traveled to the United States in 1941 to help the U.S. government set up its own radar system. The U.S. system worked great. In fact, it picked up the incoming Japanese planes that would, within an hour, attack Pearl Harbor. Unfortunately, the United States thought the planes were Allied planes and ignored them.

Sonar is a system that uses underwater sound waves to detect and locate submerged objects. It gave Allied ships and submarines the opportunity to stop the deadly surprise attacks of German **U-boats**. The Allies fought off German U-boats for 6 long years in the Atlantic Ocean. The U-boats typically targeted U.S. and especially British merchant ships as they transported supplies from the United States to British ports. The merchant ships traveled in large groups called **convoys**. Even though the merchant ships were protected by Allied warships, the Germans still managed to sink 2 million tons of Allied ships in the first 4 months of 1941 and more than 5 million tons in 1942. But in 1943, with new radar and sonar systems in place, the hunters became the hunted. In just 3 months, the Allies sank 95 U-boats and reopened Allied shipping channels. Out of 39,000 German submariners, only 11,000 survived the war.

One of the most famous U.S. inventions during World War II was the DUKW amphibious truck. Shaped like a boat, "the Duck" drove like a truck on land. With a propeller and rudder, it could also travel on water. Why were these dual-function vehicles so effective? Because they could be loaded at sea and then driven directly up the beach. This saved troops valuable time. Until these nifty vehicles were used in 1942, ships would have to load cargo into boats, reload it into trucks on shore, and then transport it to supply depots.

More than 20,000 Ducks were built during World War II to be used in the Pacific and Europe. They proved their worth during the D-day invasion of Normandy. On D-day they carried 18 million tons of soldiers and supplies ashore. The DUKW amphibious truck was developed by scientists working in the Office of Scientific Research and Development (OSRD). At first the U.S. Army didn't want the vehicles. In fact, the army took no interest in the **prototype** until engineers used it to save the lives of seven Coast Guardsmen grounded in a storm.

American engineers had invented the DC-3 in the mid-1930s, well before the war, and the C-47 was a military version of the DC-3. Known as the

★ WWII trivia ★

To reward his navy for ruthlessly hunting down the Allies, Hitler awarded the Knight's Cross to the German U-boat captains who sank more than 100,000 tons of Allied ships. Submarine "kills" were measured by the size of the ship that was sunk. Over the course of the war, hundreds of Allied ships were sunk by German U-boats. A group of German U-boats is called a wolfpack.

Definition: DUKW

What does **DUKW** stand for?

D = First year of production code; D is for 1942

U = Body style; U is for utility truck (amphibious)

K = All-wheel drive; GMC still uses that on trucks today (for example, K5 Chevy Blazer)

W = Two rear driving axles (tandem axle)

An amphibious DUKW in the Pacific.

The Fu-Go Balloon Bomb

During the war, the Japanese developed an un-manned balloon bomb, but it proved very ineffective. The so-called Fu-Go balloon bombs were launched from Japan on the prevailing winter winds. Supposedly, the winds would carry them across the Pacific and over the western United States. Mass produced by Japanese schoolchildren, the Fu-Go balloons were rigged to explode when they reached America. In all, more than 9,000 of these balloon bombs were launched, but only a few reached populated areas of the United States. The only casualties were a woman and five children in Oregon, who found one of the bombs. It exploded when they tried to pull it out of a tree.

Gooney Bird, Skytrain, or Dakota, the C-47 was built to transport soldiers, cargo, and the wounded. It could carry up to 6,000 pounds, including a fully assembled jeep or 28 soldiers dressed in full combat gear. When it ferried the wounded, the plane had enough space to hold 14 stretchers. The C-47 was so effective that every branch of the U.S. military used it during the war, as did the major Allied partners, on every continent in the world. More than 10,000 C-47 planes were built. By 1944, a new C-47 rolled off the assembly line of the Douglas Aircraft Company every 34 minutes.

The jeep was developed in America in 1940 by the Bantam Car Company based on the guidelines of U.S. Army engineers. Another company, Willys-Overland, produced the jeep for the army because Bantam was too small to manufacture the number of jeeps needed. Willys-Overland named the vehicle the Quad, but the media started calling it a jeep in 1941. The four-wheel-drive vehicle was highly effective because it could handle any type of terrain. Each vehicle could carry an 800-pound load while towing an antitank gun. War correspondent Ernie Pyle described the jeep as "faithful as a dog, strong as a mule, and agile as a goat." Because the jeep name was so well-known and well-regarded, Willys-Overland was quick to see the potential for sales to civilians after the war. So it began running advertising campaigns declaring the jeep "a powerhouse on wheels." The first civilian Jeep was produced in 1945.

Another effective, but terrifying, weapon developed by the Allies was the atomic bomb. In 1934, Leo Szilard, a Jewish scientist who had

Jeep Nicknames

peep, bug, puddle jumper, midget, pygmy, blitz buggy, Quad

left Germany for Britain in 1933, discovered that atoms could be split by bombarding them with atomic particles called neurons. This set up a chain reaction of enormous energy. Scientists in Germany, England, France, the Soviet Union, and the United States all realized the possibility of creating a large bomb from uranium. Each country raced to be the first to build it. If Germany succeeded first, the Allies knew they would be in big trouble.

In June 1942, the U.S. Army Corps of Engineers began the Manhattan Project, the secret name for the joint British and American effort to build the atomic bomb. Research was conducted by American, British, Canadian, and European scientists, some of whom were Jews who had fled Nazi Germany. More than 125,000 people worked on the Manhattan Project around the country. The Manhattan Project resulted in a working atomic bomb prototype in 1945. President Truman gave permission for two U.S. pilots to drop two atomic bombs on two Japanese cities. The pilot who dropped the bomb on Hiroshima on August 6, 1945, was Colonel Paul W. Tibbets Jr. His bomb was nicknamed "Little Boy," and his B-29 bomber was called the "*Enola Gay*," after his mother. The second bomb, nicknamed "Fat Man," was dropped on Nagasaki on August 9.

No one quite knew how much damage the bombs would cause, although scientists did know that they were 2,000 times more powerful than any bomb used in history. The results were devastating. The explosions produced ground temperatures of about 5,400 degrees Fahrenheit (3,000 degrees Celsius), which is about twice the

Enola Gay Pilot Speaks

"The *Enola Gay* has become a symbol to different groups for one reason or another. I suggest that she be preserved and given her place in the context of the times in which she flew. For decades she has been relegated to a storage facility. Her place in history has been dealt with unfairly by those who decry the inhumanity of her August 6th mission. Ladies and gentlemen, there is no humanity in warfare. The job of the combatants, the families, the diplomats, and factory workers is to win. All had a role in that 'all out' fight."

Part of a statement offered by retired U.S. Air Force Brigadier General Paul W. Tibbets at the Airmen Memorial Museum on June 8, 1994.

Top: Little Boy
Bottom: Fat Man

Barrage Balloons

During World War II, the British and U.S. governments used barrage balloons to defend against low-flying German bomber planes. These large balloons were filled with lighter-than-air gas, and anchored to the ground by a steel cable in groups or clusters. The height of the balloons could be raised or lowered with a winch operated by crews on the ground. The balloons forced enemy aircraft to fly higher, so their bombs weren't as accurate. Their cables sometimes snared enemy planes that attempted to fly lower. When the Germans developed the V-1 pilotless flying bomb and launched thousands of them toward London, the British used groups of barrage balloons to shield the city. Still, by August 1944 more than 20,000 London residents had been killed or injured by the "doodlebugs" and more than a million houses damaged. Although the United States was not threatened by direct air attack at any time during the war, six balloon squadrons were formed to protect naval bases and depots. American barrage balloons were operated by the U.S. Army and U.S. Marine Corps.

melting point of iron. A huge shock wave crushed objects, and created powerful winds that spread dangerous radioactive particles through the air. These particles fell on the ground, contaminating animals and humans. More than 110,000 Japanese civilians died immediately. Many thousands more died painful deaths from radiation-induced sickness. The world was quick to decide it did not want nuclear bombs used in the future, although the United States and some other countries continue to have nuclear weapons. Did any good come about because of the bombs? Yes. Japan immediately surrendered to the Allies, quickly ending the war. The quick end to the war saved many lives on both sides.

⭐ WWII trivia ⭐

After World War II, Japan became a democracy, even though Emperor Hirohito, considered a "god-king" by the Japanese people, was allowed to remain on the throne. All Japanese men and women were given equal rights. The United States occupied Japan for nearly 7 years after the war and helped the Japanese to get back on their feet. By 1955, 10 years after the end of the war, Japan was a leader in modern manufacturing.

Technology played an important role in World War II, but it is important to recognize that technology alone cannot win a war. The outcome of the war could have been very different. The Allies were also helped by weather, timing, plentiful resources, a strong workforce, and lots of luck.

Make Your Own
Barrage Balloon Flotilla

During World War I, the British formed barrage balloon "aprons" by placing three balloons 500 yards apart. In World War II the British used thousands! In this activity you'll use blown eggs and foil to create a miniature barrage balloon flotilla.

1 First you'll blow the eggs clean. Shake each egg, which helps to break up the yolk so it is easier to blow out. Make a hole in each end of the raw egg with a needle. Use a toothpick to make one of the holes wider. You can also use the toothpick to break the egg yolk in several places by sticking it deep into the egg. Stand over a bowl and blow hard into the small hole, which will force the yolk out the larger hole. Keep blowing until the egg is empty. Repeat with the other eggs. Wash the eggs well, then let them dry.

2 Cut the top off the egg carton, then cover it with either green or brown construction paper. This serves as your dirt or grass. The top of the carton should be facing up.

3 From the bottom of the carton, cut a tail and two fins for each egg. Carefully attach these parts to the back end of each egg with tape. (See diagram for placement.)

4 Take a piece of the foil and gently wrap your egg to give it the distinctive silver coloring of a barrage balloon. The thin foil is easy to manipulate around the tail and fins and make smooth. The foil will also keep the tail and fins in place.

5 Use the needle to carefully punch a hole in the belly of the egg. Put one end of the skewer into the hole, using glue to secure it if it does not catch in the foil. Place the other end of the skewer through the egg carton top. Space the three eggs equally to form a barrage balloon flotilla!

supplies

- ✪ **6 raw eggs**
- ✪ **sewing needle**
- ✪ **toothpick**
- ✪ **egg carton**
- ✪ **scissors**
- ✪ **brown or green construction paper**
- ✪ **glue**
- ✪ **clear tape**
- ✪ **thin foil**
- ✪ **6 wooden skewers**

tail

fins

GLOSSARY

A

Allies: The countries that fought together against Hitler and the Axis Powers during World War II, particularly Britain, the United States, France, and the Soviet Union.

amphibious: Belonging or working on both land and water.

anti-Semitism: Prejudice against Jews.

atomic bomb: An extremely powerful bomb dropped on two Japanese cities to end World War II. Also called a nuclear bomb.

atomic energy: Energy released by changes in the nucleus of an atom.

Axis Powers: The countries that fought against the Allied forces during World War II, primarily Germany, Japan, and Italy.

B

bazooka: A lightweight rocket launcher, held on the shoulder. It was an important antitank weapon for U.S. soldiers.

black market: The illegal sale or purchase of items officially controlled by the government.

Blitz, the: The period from September 1940 to May 1941 when the German air force bombed London and other British cities. The most intense period of bombing was for 57 straight nights starting on September 7, 1940. By the end of the Blitz, 2 million British houses had been destroyed and 60,000 civilians had been killed.

C

casualties: People killed, wounded, captured, or missing in action in a war.

chaos: Confusion.

code talkers: Members of the Comanche and Navajo tribes who helped the U.S. military to send and receive coded messages. The code was based on their native languages.

concentration camps: Harsh labor camps set up by the Nazis to confine Jews and other people they deemed inferior or enemies of Germany. Some concentration camps, like Auschwitz, were extermination camps where prisoners were sent to be killed.

counterespionage: The discovery and defeat of enemy espionage.

cryptogram: A text written in code.

cryptology: The study of codes; the art of writing and solving them.

cipher: A method of putting text in code to hide its meaning, like writing 1 for A, 2 for B, etc., or F for A, S for B.

D

D-day: The first day of any military operation. The most famous D-day was June 6, 1944, when the Allied forces invaded France to liberate it from Germany.

decode: To convert a message in code back into ordinary language.

democracy: Government based on equality and majority rule.

deploy: To go to the battlefield.

dictator: A ruler who exerts total control over a society.

discrimination: Treating someone differently because of race, gender, or other characteristic.

draft: To recruit or force a person to serve in the military.

DUKW: An amphibious military truck used during World War II.

E

encode: To transfer information from one system of communication into another.

Enigma: The coded message machine used by the Germans during World War II.

espionage: Spying.

F

fascism: Government by a dictator who rules through terror.

Fat Man: The atomic bomb that was dropped by a U.S. B-29 bomber plane on Nagasaki, Japan, on August 9, 1945. Approximately 35,000 people died.

front line: A military line formed by the most advanced tactical units in a combat situation, or the line or zone of contact with an enemy.

G

ghetto: A section of a city in which people are forced to live. The Nazis forced Jews into ghettos.

GI: A nickname for a U.S. soldier, from the words "government issue."

H

Hiroshima: The Japanese city destroyed on August 6, 1945, when the United States dropped the first atomic bomb ever used in warfare.

Hitler Youth: A mandatory youth club for German boys. Founded by the Nazi party, it taught Nazi ideas, especially the hatred of Jewish people.

Holocaust, the: The Nazi program of exterminating Jews between 1941 and 1945. More than 6 million European Jews were murdered at concentration camps, as well as 5–6 million others.

home front: Civilian activity supporting the army of a nation at war. This involves production and supply of war supplies, civilian defense, and maintaining public order and morale.

I

inflation: A rise in prices.

intelligence: Information about an enemy.

Isolationism: A policy of not getting involved in political or economic relations with other countries. Before Pearl Harbor many in the U.S. government wanted to remain uninvolved.

Issei: A term used by the Japanese to mean "first generation." The Issei were Japanese immigrants who were not able to become American citizens because of laws passed in the 1920s.

J

Japanese Relocation Centers: Isolated and guarded internment camps where Japanese Americans living on the West Coast after the bombing of Pearl Harbor were forced to live.

K

kamikaze: Japanese suicide pilots who crashed explosive-packed planes into enemy ships, killing thousands of Allied soldiers. Kamikaze means "divine wind."

Kristallnacht: The night of November 9, 1938, when the Nazis coordinated an attack on Jewish people and their property in Germany and German-controlled lands.

L

Lend-Lease Act: The legislation that allowed President Roosevelt to send money and equipment to the Allies to help fight the war.

Little Boy: The atomic bomb dropped on Hiroshima by the United States on August 6, 1945. The explosion killed 80,000 Japanese citizens.

Luftwaffe: The German air force.

M

morale: A sense of purpose and usefulness; confidence in the future.

N

Nagasaki: The second Japanese city devastated by an atomic bomb launched by the United States. After this bombing, which occurred on August 9, 1945, Japan surrendered, ending World War II.

Nazi Party: Another name for the National Socialist German Workers' Party, founded in Germany in 1919 and brought to power in 1933 when Adolf Hitler was appointed Chancellor. Hitler then established a totalitarian dictatorship.

Nisei: A Japanese term that means "second generation." These Japanese Americans were born in the United States, which means they were U.S. citizens. Their rights, however, were swept away after the Japanese attack on Pearl Harbor.

Nuremberg Laws: In 1935, the Nazis passed a number of laws that deprived German Jews of their rights of citizenship, forbade them to marry non-Jews, and classified a Jew as someone who had three Jewish grandparents. Even if these people were not practicing Judaism, or had converted to Christianity, the Nazis still classified them as Jews—and viewed them as enemies of Germany.

Nuremberg Trials: After the war, 22 of Nazi Germany's leaders were brought to trial in Nuremberg, Germany, for war crimes and crimes against humanity. Twelve were sentenced to death.

O

Office of Price Administration (OPA): A government agency that set ration levels and price controls during World War II.

Office of Scientific Research and Development: The government agency charged with developing technologies that would help the Allies during the war.

Operation Overlord: The code name for the Allied invasion of Normandy, France.

P

Pearl Harbor: The U.S. naval base that the Japanese bombed in 1941. This act caused the United States to officially enter the war.

POW: Prisoner of war.

prejudice: Hostility toward a race or group.

propaganda: Information that is spread for the purpose of promoting a cause. During World War II governments used propaganda to motivate soldiers and civilians to be patriotic.

Purple cipher: The name of the coded message machine developed and used by the Japanese during World War II.

R

radar: A system for locating an object with radio signals.

rationing: To restrict the consumption of something scarce.

ration kit: Pre-made meals the military uses to feed troops in the field.

recycle: The process of extracting useful materials from a variety of items for the purpose of reuse. During the war, the government recycled metal, rubber, nylon, and other items to make war supplies.

refugee: A person who flees in search of refuge, as in times of war or religious persecution. Many Jews fled Nazi Germany before and during World War II.

Resistance, the: An organized movement in a conquered country to sabotage the invaders.

Rosie the Riveter: A fictional character representing the 6 million women who worked in factories that made war supplies during World War II.

S

sabotage: The deliberate act of damaging equipment, materials, premises, or utilities used for war or national defense.

scapegoat: A person blamed for the mistakes, failures, or wrongdoings of others.

segregation: Separation of the races.

sonar: A device that detects the presence and location of an object under water.

Star of David: A Jewish symbol with six points symbolizing God's rule over the universe in all directions: north, south, east, west, up, and down. It is made by overlapping two triangles.

surveillance: To observe or watch someone.

swastika: The emblem of the Nazi party and of the German state under Adolf Hitler, although the Nazis did not create the symbol.

T

Third Reich: The German state from 1933 to 1945 under Adolf Hitler. The life of the Third Reich was far shorter than the 1,000 years that Hitler had predicted before his death.

Tripartite Pact: The agreement signed by Germany, Italy, and Japan on September 27, 1940, which formed the Axis Powers. The three powers agreed to stand by each other for 10 years.

troops: A group of soldiers.

U

U-boat: A German submarine.

United Service Organizations (USO): A program established by President Franklin Roosevelt to support and entertain U.S. troops. The funds for USOs came from private donations.

V

veteran: A person who has served in the armed forces, in a time of war or peace.

V-E Day: May 8, 1945, the day the Allies announced the surrender of German forces in Europe.

victory garden: Gardens that were planted by American civilians during World War II. About 2 million gardens produced 40 percent of the food grown in the United States during the war.

V-J Day: August 15, 1945, the day the Allies announced the surrender of Japanese forces during World War II. Japan formally signed the surrender on September 2.

V-mail: The format of mail sent to U.S. troops fighting on the battlefront during World War II. Letters were photographed and the film sent overseas because it was lighter than paper. Once at its destination, the film was printed out and sent to the recipient.

W

war bonds: Savings bonds issued by the U.S. government to finance the war effort. The bonds also helped to manage inflation by removing money from the economy.

War Refugee Board (WRB): An agency set up by President Roosevelt in 1944 to attempt to rescue Jewish refugees in German-occupied Europe. Although it helped to save about 200,000 Jews, millions had already been killed in Nazi concentration camps.

War Relocation Authority (WRA): U.S. civilian agency responsible for the relocation and internment of Japanese Americans during World War II. The WRA was created by President Roosevelt on March 18, 1942, with Executive Order 9102 and officially ceased to exist on June 30, 1946.

World War I: The First World War, fought between 1914 and 1918.

RESOURCES

BOOKS

Aaseng, Nathan. *Navajo Code Talkers*. New York: Walker Publishing Company, Inc., 1992.

Baker, Patricia. *Fashions of a Decade: The 1940s.* New York: Facts on File, 1992.

Cooper, Michael L. *Fighting for Honor: Japanese Americans and World War II*. New York: Clarion Books, 2000.

Frank, Anne. *The Diary of a Young Girl: The Definitive Edition.* New York: Doubleday, 1995.

Hayes, Joanne Lamb. *Grandma's Wartime Kitchen: World War II and the Way We Cooked*. New York: St. Martin's Press, 2000.

King, David C. *World War II Days: Discover the Past with Exciting Projects, Games, Activities, and Recipes*. New York: John Wiley & Sons, Inc., 2000.

Kuhn, Betsy. *Angels of Mercy: the Army Nurses of World War II*. New York: Atheneum Books for Young Readers, 1999.

Lawton, Clive A. *Hiroshima: The Story of the First Atom Bomb*. Cambridge, MA: Candlewick Press, 2004.

Lingeman, Richard. *Don't You Know There's a War On? The American Home Front, 1941–1945*, updated edition. New York: Nation Books, 2003.

Morin, Isobel V. *Days of Judgment: The World War II War Crimes Trials*. Brookfield, CT: Millbrook Press, 1995.

Panchyk, Richard. *World War II for Kids*. Chicago: Chicago Review Press, 2002.

UNIVERSITY AND GOVERNMENT SITES

National Museum of the United States Air Force—http://www.wpafb.af.mil/museum/index.htm

National Museum of the United States Army—http://www.armyhistory.org/index.aspx

National WWII Memorial—http://www.wwiimemorial.com

United States Holocaust Memorial Museum—http://www.ushmm.org/museum

PHOTO CREDITS:

Pg. IV: Hitler (captured German photo), and Pg. V: Tojo (captured Japanese film): courtesy of Patrick Clancey, www.ibiblio.org/hyperwar/index.html; Pg. IV: Roosevelt: CIA photo; Pg. V: Eisenhower: NATO photo; Pg. 13: V-J Day office radio: Minnesota Historical Society; Pg. 14: dancers: Simon Selmon and Taina Kortelainen, photo by Tony Rusecki; Pg. 16: Anderson Shelter, and Pg. 18: Morrison Shelter: courtesy of Peter Risbey; Pg. 21: Supermarine Spitfire, and Pg. 73: Auschwitz: courtesy of Wikipedia; Pg. 40: victory garden: courtesy of Norfolk Public Library; Pg. 40: poster: courtesy of Northwestern Public Library; Pg. 42: dress patterns: courtesy of www.woodland-farmsantiques.com; Pg. 52: TV: courtesy of Tom Genova, www.tvhistory.tv; Pg. 72: Walkie Talkie: courtesy of David Hollander; Pg. 78: enigma cipher machine: courtesy of www.w1tp.com/enigma; Pg. 81: Navajo code talkers: U.S. Marine Corps photo, courtesy of DefenseLINK; Pg. 84: DUKW: courtesy of U.S. Army Quartermaster Museum; Pg. 92: care package drive: U.S. Air Force photo by Linda LaBonte Britt; Pg. 94: P-51 Mustang: courtesy of Dave Key, www.militaryairshows.co.uk; Pg. 99: WAAC uniforms: courtesy of The U.S. Army Women's Museum, Ft. Lee, Virginia; Pg. 104: Panzer tank: photo by Rod Larson; Pg. 107: amphibious DUKW: courtesy of U.S. Army Quartermaster Museum; Pg. 108: Jeep: courtesy of Atterbury-Bakalar Air Museum; Pg. 109: Little Boy and Fat Man Bombs: courtesy of U.S. Department of Defense; **From the Library of Congress:** Pg. IV: Stalin; and Stalin, Roosevelt, Churchill (American memory collection); Pg. V: Churchill and Eisenhower; and Truman; Pg. 8: Japanese children; Pg. 36: community canning center (WPA collection, by Howard Hollem); Pg. 96: 442nd Infantry; Pg. 50: GI Joe poster; Pg. 58: boys at fence, and portrait of man (by Ansel Adams); Pg. 110: barrage balloon; **From the U.S. National Archives:** Pg. 8: Pearl Harbor; Pg. 9: D-Day landing; Pg. 10: New York City kiss; Pg. 43: beauty parlor; Pg. 63: Paris bombing; Pg. 85: basketball on USS Monterey; Pg. 88: Tokyo Rose; Pg. 93: black aviator; Pg. 94: Tuskegee airmen.

INDEX